Quick Gifts

handmade with care

The suggestions contained in this book have been carefully developed and tested by the author and the publisher. However, no guarantees can be made. The author and/or publisher and their agents bear no responsibility for any physical or monetary damages.

© 2005/IMP BV
© for this English edition:
Naumann & Göbel Verlagsgesellschaft mbH, a subsidiary of
VEMAG Verlags- und Medien Aktiengesellschaft, Cologne
www.apollo-intermedia.de

Complete production:
Naumann & Göbel Verlagsgesellschaft mbH, Cologne
Printed in Germany

All rights reserved
ISBN 3-625-11653-7

Quick Gifts

handmade with care

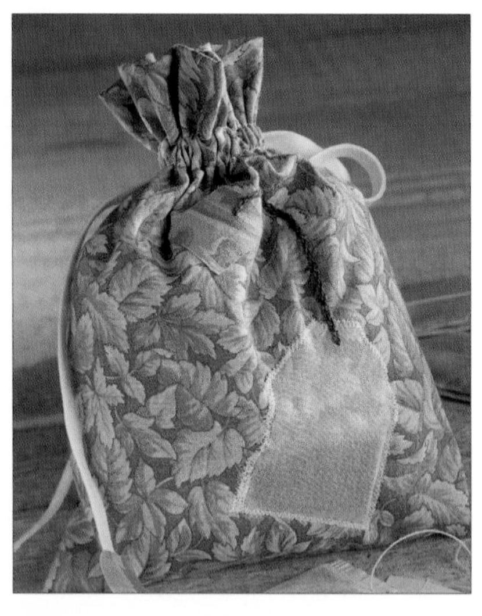

Contents

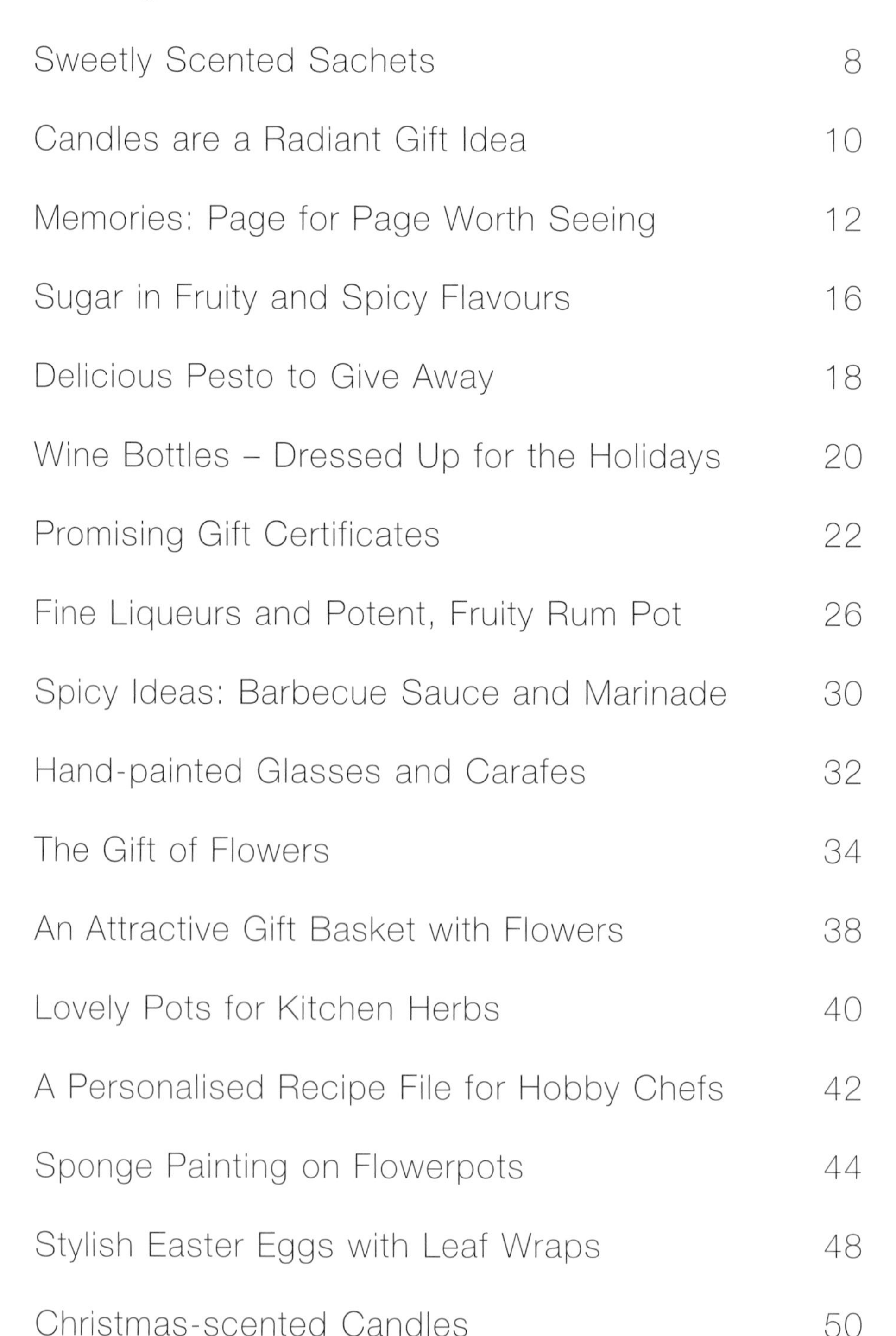

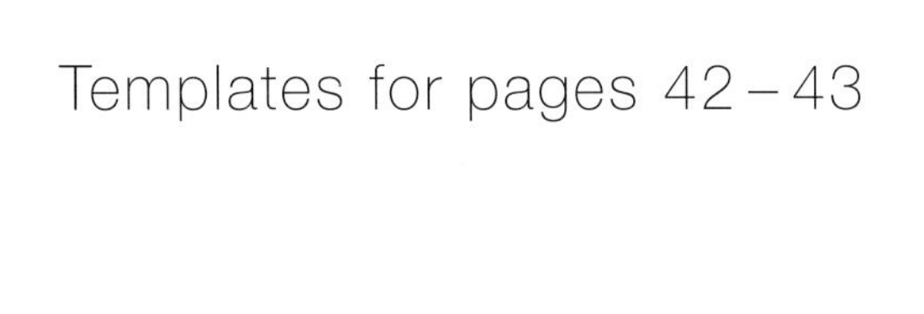

Use part of the bag's contents for decoration. For example, stitch up a tea bag and fill it with real tea. If you decide to make a potpourri sachet instead, you can sew a tiny pouch made of lace that contains a dried flower onto the sachet.

Gift Bags for Coffee and Tea

The ideal present for the connoisseur. Fill bags you sew yourself from a suitable material with roasted coffee beans or an aromatic tea.

Any coffee or tea lover will be thrilled to receive this gift. The cloth bags can be used again and again to store other items. They are made from coarse sacking and are reminiscent of the large burlap sacks that are used to ship coffee beans around the globe. Decorate the front of the bag with a fitting motif, such as coffee beans, using brown fabric. Stitch a channel about one inch from the top of the bag, then thread a ribbon or drawstring through it in order to tie the bag shut.

You can make the bags any size you like. Select a fabric or material that is suited to the content: for example, a bag made of burlap is especially well-suited for coffee beans, while a bag made of a thicker weave, patterned fabric is more appropriate to hold tea.

The first step is to sew the narrow sides of the fabric together, leaving 10 cm free at the top. You will use this fabric later to create the channel for the drawstring and the top. Then sew the bottom of the bag together. It will look better if you sew a side stitch in the back rear panel before machine-stitching the lower edge.

Once the bag is sewn, secure the decorative motifs to the front of the bag. Make sure you don't position them too high, because you will next sew a drawstring channel at the top. Draw a suitable drawstring or ribbon through the channel. Tie a knot at both ends to make sure the drawstring does not fray. You can also decorate the ends of the drawstring, for example, by sewing pieces of fabric shaped as coffee beans or even a small tea bag onto the ends.

Material

- **Fabric**
- **Ribbon or drawstring**
- **Two-sided, adhesive interfacing**
- **Mercerised or cotton yarn**
- **Tea or coffee**
- **Measuring tape**
- **Pencil**
- **Scissors**
- **Needle and thread**
- **Safety pin**
- **Embroidery needle**
- **Sewing machine**
- **Iron**
- **Teaspoon**

How to Sew a Beautiful Coffee Gift Bag

1 Iron adhesive interfacing onto brown material. Draw and cut out coffee bean halves. Cut burlap into 50 x 30 cm rectangles, making sure it is lint-free. Pin the pieces, right sides together.

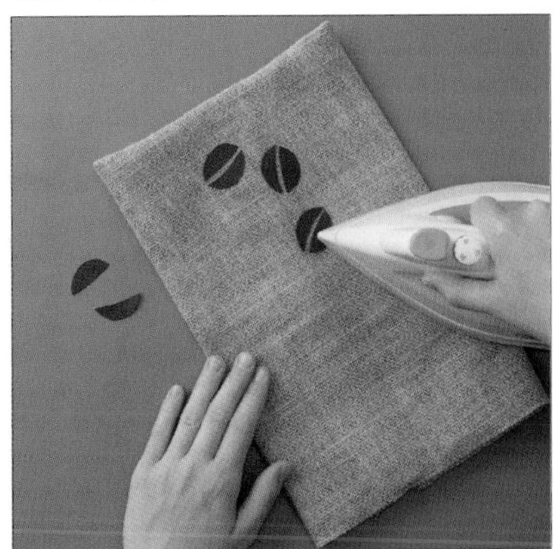

2 Machine-stitch the narrow edges and bottom, leaving 10 cm open at the top. Remove the protective plastic of the interfacing and iron the coffee beans to the front of the bag, leaving space for the drawstring.

3 Turn 5 cm of the top edge down and stitch it 2.5 cm and 4 cm from the edge. This will create a 1.5-cm-wide drawstring channel.

4 Use the safety pin to draw the ribbon or drawstring through the channel. Fill the bag with coffee or tea, pull the drawstring, and tie a bow.

How to Create a Gift Bag for Tea

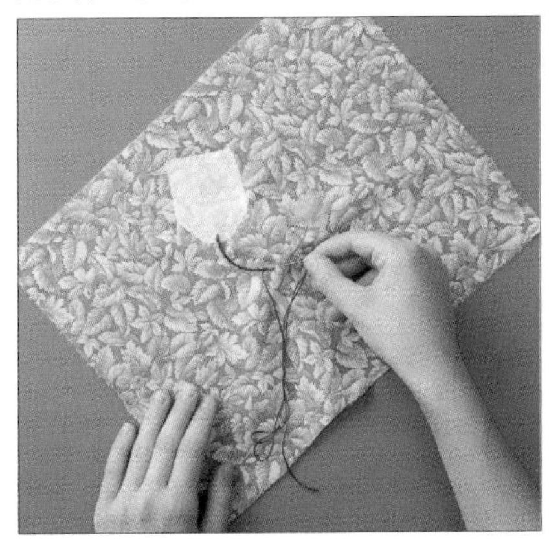

1 Sew thin, white fabric as a tea bag onto a 30 x 25 cm piece of fabric. Leave the top open. Affix the square using adhesive interfacing, then stitch the string with embroidery thread.

2 Fill the pouch with tea, then close top. Stitch the bag sides and bottom, leaving 5 cm open at the top, then sew two rows for the drawstring channel and draw ribbon or string through it.

Fabric handkerchiefs with beautiful lace trimming are especially well-suited for creating nostalgic scented pillows and sachets. Place some potpourri in the middle of the handkerchief, gather the corners together and tie them together with some ribbon. You can also decorate clothes hangers in the same fabric to match the sachets, for example.

Sweetly Scented Sachets

Sachets are a novel gift idea that you can stitch together in no time at all to create a small, thoughtful present. They keep your clothes and your cupboard smelling fresh.

You can use special fabric such as silk organza or fabric with an interesting structure for these creations, but these sachets look beautiful even when made with a simple floral print on cotton. Decorate your sachets with ribbon, lace, and embroidery and fill them with a delightful and fragrant potpourri mixture of lavender or roses. You can easily create your own scented blend from dried flowers and aromatic oils.

If you are sewing the sachets from organza, it is best to double the fabric since it is very transparent. If you are using stronger fabric, such as a cotton floral print, one layer will suffice.

Please keep in mind that the colour of the potpourri will be visible through the organza. If your potpourri has a lot of green or woody tones to it, it may show through the fabric and dominate the softer pastel tones of the fabric. In this case, you should use a potpourri of dried flowers and other dried materials whose colours harmonise with the fabric. You will need approximately 12 cm of fabric with a width of 115 cm for one sachet.

You can find broderie anglaise and other embroidered decorations to sew onto the sachets in large fabric stores, in warehouses and in well-stocked haberdasheries. When placed in the middle of the sachet, small decorative embroidery is a beautiful addition that draws one's eye. Sew them on with a sewing machine and a small zigzag stitch, making sure that you do not stretch the thin fabric.

There are many beautiful ribbons and braid trimming available. Select a ribbon that harmonises with the fabric or one in a contrasting colour.

- **Silk organza**
- **Fabric with broderie anglaise or embroidered decorations**
- **Scissors**
- **Measuring tape**
- **Pins**
- **Sewing thread**
- **Sewing machine**
- **Iron**
- **Ribbons**
- **Potpourri**

How to Sew a Romantic Sachet

1 Iron the organza using a low temperature setting. Fold the fabric lengthwise in the middle and cut it into 12-cm-wide strips. Fold again, measure two 41-cm-long sections on the long side and cut.

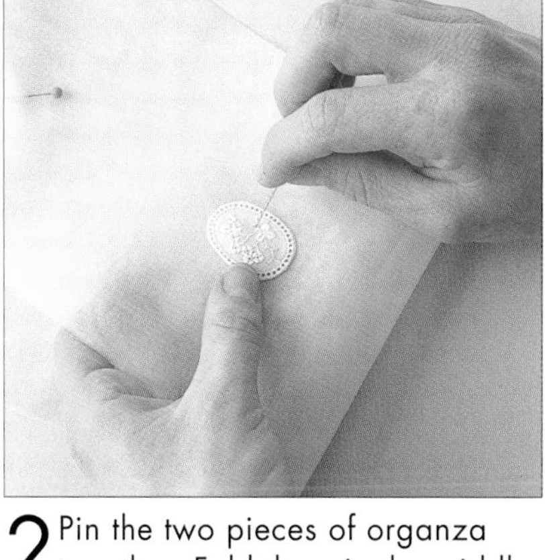

2 Pin the two pieces of organza together. Fold them in the middle horizontally and position the embroidered motif in the middle of the bottom half. Position the fabric so it is flat and pin the motif in place.

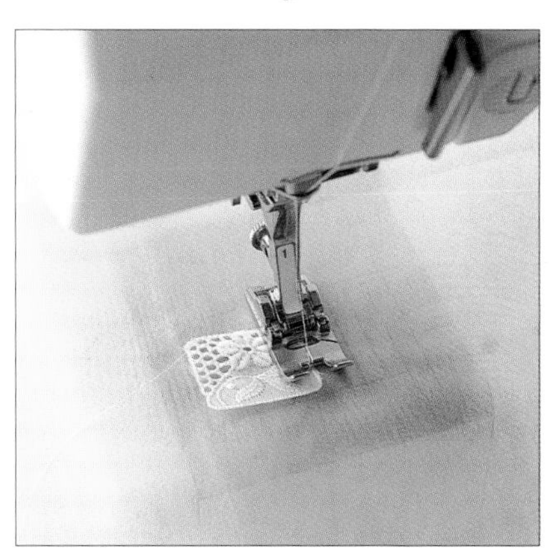

3 Set the sewing machine to a small zigzag stitch, with a width of 2 and a length of 1.5. Test the stitch on a fabric remnant. Carefully sew the embroidered motif onto the fabric by hand.

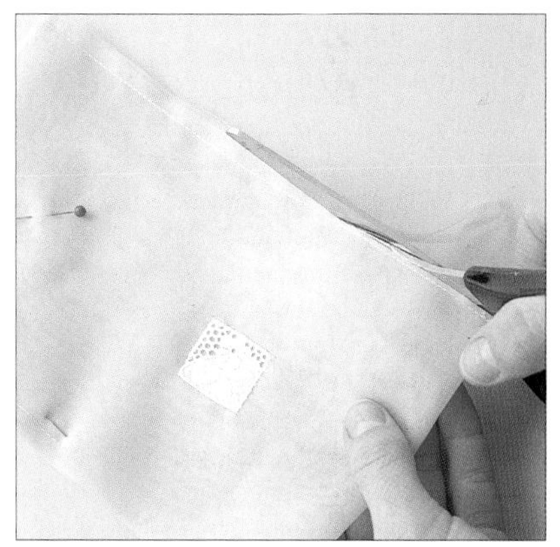

4 Fold the strips of fabric horizontally in half with the wrong sides facing each other and machine-stitch a straight stitch along both sides, close to the edge. Cut off the extra material close to the stitching.

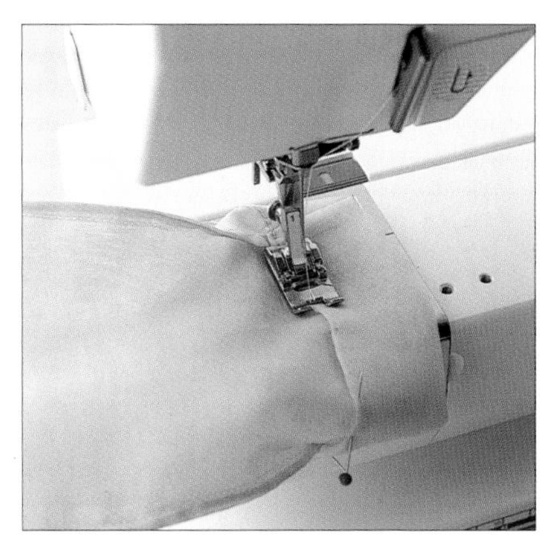

5 Turn the sachet inside out and iron the edges. Machine-stitch both long sides close to the edge. Turn down 5 cm at the top, hem the cut edge, pin the seam, and sew.

6 Turn the sachet right-side out and fill it with the potpourri. Cut the ribbon to the desired length and tie up the sachet opening with the ribbon. Tie a bow.

Depending on the occasion and the tastes of the intended recipient, you can decorate candles in wide a variety of ways. Simple things that you have at home are often all you need to put together creative gifts.

Candles are a Radiant Gift Idea

Candles that are embellished and cleverly bundled together are a wonderful hostess gift to bring to a party instead of flowers.

Unusual ribbons and various decorative materials emphasise the form of the slender candles and are practical since they keep them bundled together at the same time. For example, you can use herbs or spices, leaves, twigs, sprigs of berries or the like and combine them with a large, colourful ribbon or cord for an interesting decoration. With a little bit of imagination and different materials you will come up with the most wonderful ideas and turn candles into great gifts.

Take three or more simple candles and bundle them together. The bundle will have a more pleasing shape if you use an odd number of candles. In order to make it easier to decorate the candles, you should hold them together with some clear tape that will no longer be visible under the decoration. Use your imagination to gather together decorative items for the candles.

If you use a narrow ribbon or a thin cord, it is a good idea to wrap it around the candles several times, since they will hold together better and also look nicer. If you use a wide ribbon you will have plenty of room to glue various decorations onto it. For example, many herbs and berries, which smell lovely and are also appealing to the eye, are especially well-suited for this. Glue them directly in the centre of the ribbon so that they are positioned in the middle of the candles when you wrap the bow around the bundle. Make sure the ribbon lays smooth around the candles and tuck in small branches, twigs, sprigs or leaves after you have wrapped the ribbon around the candles. This way you can easily position decorative greens or boughs of berries on and around the ribbon.

Material

- **Candles**
- **Transparent tape**
- **Decorative ribbon or cording**
- **Glue**
- **Herbs**
- **Leaves**

Candles with Ribbon and Ginger

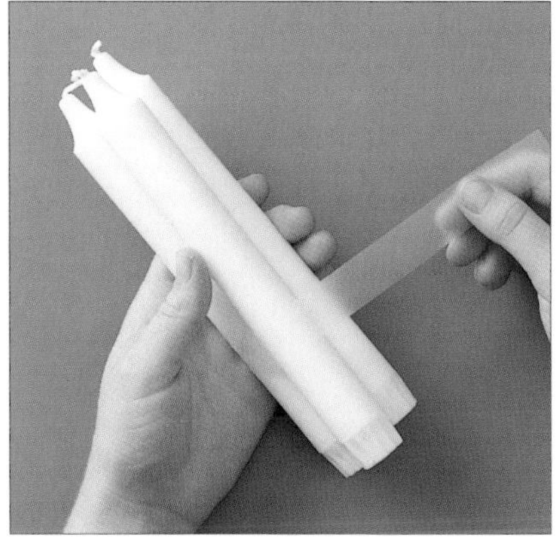

1 Gather several candles together. Make sure they are all the same size and none of them is taller than the others. Tape the bundle together where you want to position the decorative ribbon later.

2 Using wide decorative ribbon, cut a piece long enough to be wrapped around the candles twice, and have enough for a bow. Glue dried ginger to the middle of the ribbon. Let the glue dry.

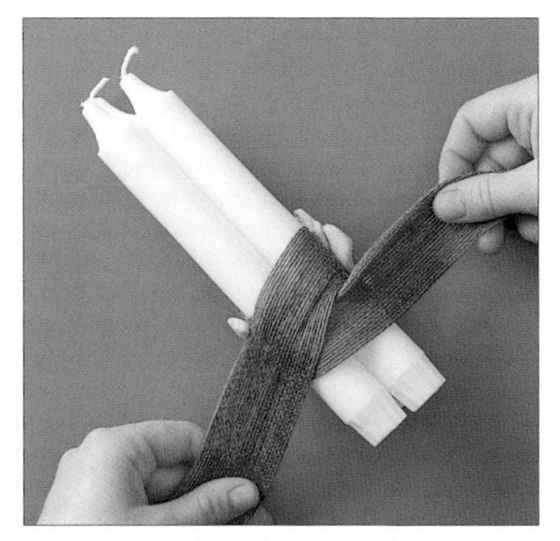

3 Position the ribbon on the candles with the ginger at the front and centre. Wrap the ribbon twice around the candles.

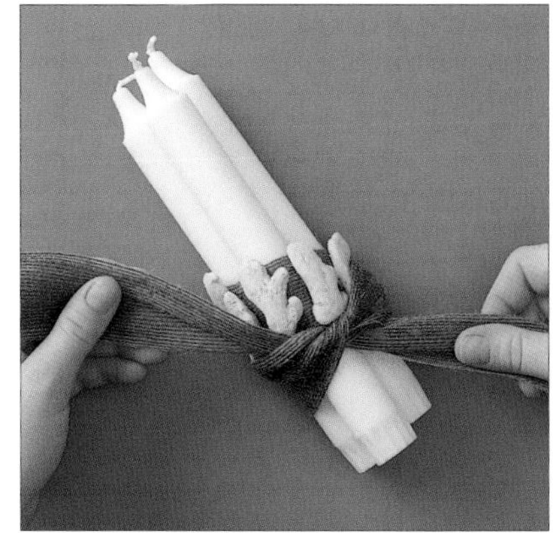

4 Carefully position the ribbon, tying it just below the ginger, and tie a decorative bow.

Candles with Cord and Leaves

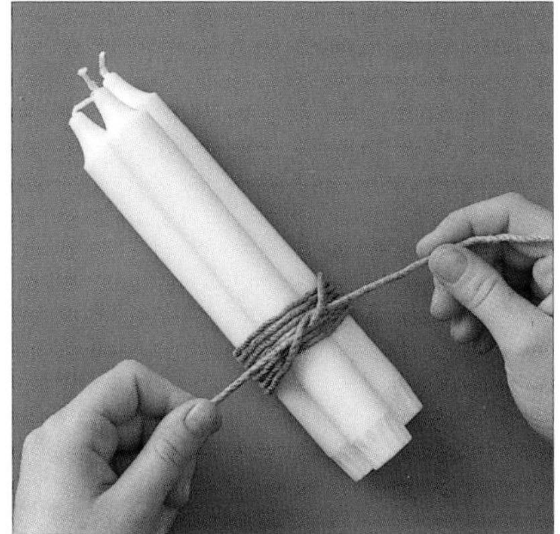

1 Wrap a simple cord around the bundle of candles several times. Pull the cord tight, tie a knot, and tie a bow in the middle.

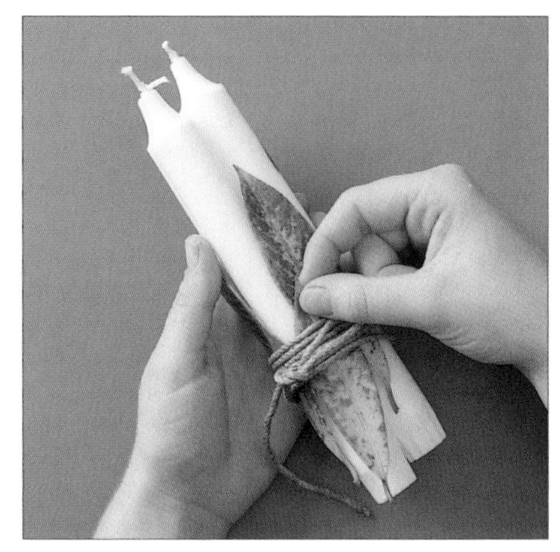

2 Tuck leaves into the cording. Distribute the leaves evenly, allowing them to overlap somewhat so that there are no gaps.

Black card cut to size is a very effective background for photos. You can carefully mount them on the card with small adhesive photo corners. An album made from recycled newspaper can be decorated with a fancy label. The sky's the limit!

Memories: Page for Page Worth Seeing

Photo albums are a very unique gift in which you can gather together pictures from a wedding, your last vacation, or other special events – what a wonderful idea!

You can create your very own unique albums using cardstock or another sturdy material, creating a photo album that is made-to-order in every respect. An album for wedding pictures might be elegant, while an album for vacation snapshots can shine in bold colours. Create the album based on the size of the photos. You can also mount and frame each photo using colours that match the images. Each photo album will be a one-of-a-kind gift!

When making your own photo album, it is important to use a relatively thick piece of cardstock. Make sure your scissors are extremely sharp, because that is the only way to ensure your corners are cut perfectly square. Select card for a decorative cover and affix as many photo pockets as you want – and your album will be ready to fill! Two pictures fit on each page, so you will only need half as many pockets as you have pictures. Finely grooved corrugated card, which you can buy in specialty paper stores, can be an ideal album cover.

Choose paper that is sturdy but not too thick for the photo mounts, and use thinner paper for the white page dividers.

You can use the templates on pages 52–55 to cut out the pages. The dimensions of the album were created to fit a standard picture format of 10 x 15 cm. If you want to use different size photos, simply adapt the dimensions to fit your photos. You can extend the cover using the dotted lines to double the size of the pages.

Material

- **Thick card**
- **Thin card**
- **White paper**
- **Glue or adhesive**
- **String or cording**
- **Ruler**
- **Pencil**
- **Sharp knife**
- **Scissors**
- **Hole punch**
- **Templates on pages 52–55**

1 Double the dimensions of the dotted line on the long side of the cover (it is black on the template). Trace them onto the cardstock and cut out the card.

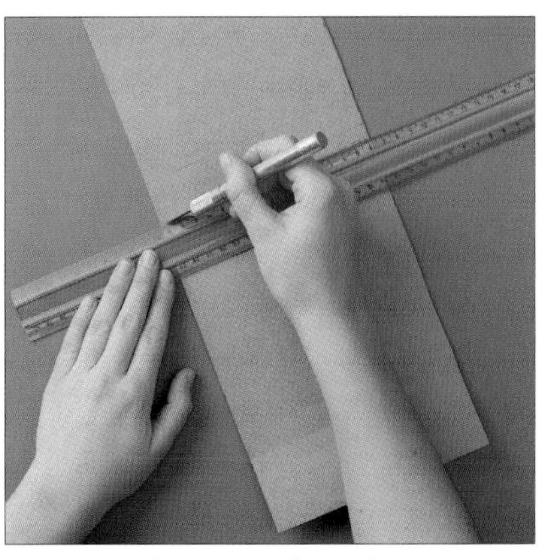

2 Trace the marks from the template for the spine of the cover; it should be 1 cm wide. Crease the card on both sides with the help of a sharp knife so that you can fold the cover.

3 Select a colourful piece of card for a photo mount. Double the dimensions (the blue line on the template) and cut it out accordingly. Trace the inside rectangle.

4 Carefully fold the photo mount in the middle. Position the ruler along the sides of the rectangle and cut out a window using a sharp knife. Be extra careful when cutting out the corners.

5 Cut white paper to create the dividers. The pages should be a little smaller than the photo mounts (for example, 18 x 14 cm). If you want them to be sturdier, you can also use thin card.

6 Apply a thin layer of glue to the bottom and sides of the photo mount, leaving the top free. Lay a divider on one side and fold the other side on top. Follow the same steps for the other photo mount pages.

7 Crimp the card about 2 cm from the back edge with a sharp knife so that you can fold the album page. Trace the markings from the template with a pencil.

8 Draw marks for the holes onto the narrow side of the cover. Punch holes in the cover with a hole punch. With a pencil, mark the locations for the holes on the pages under the cover.

The photographs will be protected by the wide photo mount, but you may want to do something different to display your photos. Cut pieces of transparent plastic somewhat larger than the window and glue the pieces in the frame on both sides of the window before you glue in the white dividers. You can hold the individual pages together using a cord that matches the colours in your photos.

9 Punch holes in all the album pages according to the markings on the template. Position the pages between the covers, pull string or cording through the holes from the outside, and knot well.

If you do not have a lot of time to make an attractive album from beginning to end, simply cut your own cover from card and use plastic photo envelopes to hold the pictures. You will have a practical album that has a lot of room for pictures in no time. Specialty shops offer a large variety of premade photo pages.

A Special Album for Grandma

You can effortlessly create a beautiful album that is reminiscent of the past using natural-coloured card. We have included a template for oval and square windows at the back of this book. If you have photos of other sizes, you can easily adapt them to fit your photos.

You will need two sheets of paper for each album page: one that you can cut for the photo mount and one for the backing. The pages are bound with a ribbon, and you can easily change the photos without a lot of effort. Affix the photos with adhesive photo corners.

Double the dimensions of the album cover and trace the outline on a piece of sturdy cardstock. Add 1 cm on the edges and 1 cm for the fold on the edge. Cut the card and crease the edge lines.

Mark the holes on the album pages and on the card cover and punch them out with a hole punch. The album will be held together with a matching ribbon.

An album that recalls days gone by, yet especially practical: to exchange the photos all you need to do is untie the little bows. The oval and square openings provide a lovely frame your pictures.

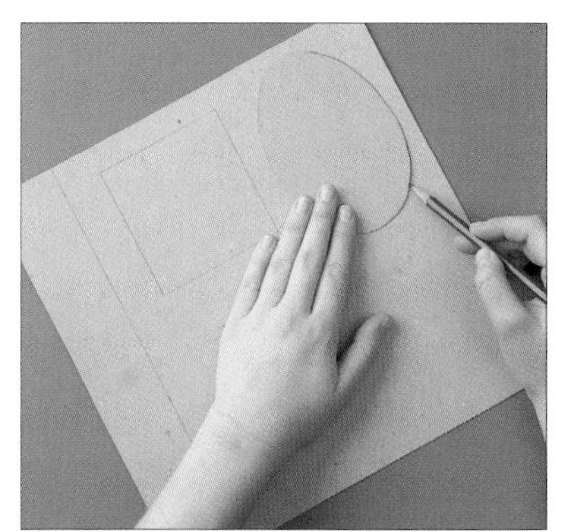

1 Trace the dimensions from the template onto the card with the various photo openings, or draw a window that suits your needs. Carefully cut out the windows.

2 Punch holes in the centre of the front and back albulm covers with the hole punch. Thread an approx. 10-cm-long piece of thin cording through the holes and tie a small bow.

3 The cover should be 1–2 cm larger than the album pages. You should also add 1 cm for the fold. Punch holes in the pages and bind everything together.

Use the delicious sugar in various baked goods and sweets. Grog, hot tea, and cold drinks taste even better with the addition of aromatic sugar.

Sugar in Fruity and Spicy Flavours

Delicacies from your kitchen that are pleasing to the eye as well as the palate are ideal gifts. These sugar mixes are a welcome treat for people with a sweet tooth as well as tea drinkers and hobby bakers.

A large glass container filled with flavoured sugar looks especially festive. You can find just the right jar or glass in specialty stores. Simple glass containers are just as suitable as decoratively shaped ones. When you decorate the front by binding a leaf around the screw top lid, even a simple glass jar becomes an ornament. The alluring aroma of the sugar will waft up when the lid is opened – irresistable.

For these sugar mixtures, you will need extra-fine castor sugar that is easy to sift, spices, and sterile, airtight glass containers with screw tops.

You can cut dried vanilla beans lengthwise with a paring knife and add it to the sugar in the glass container. The sugar will take on the potent vanilla aroma in about three weeks.

Cinnamon sticks also give off a strong aroma and are a good choice to add to sugar. Cut the sticks lengthwise and distribute evenly throughout the sugar.

You can make orange and lemon sugar by thinly peeling the fruit and drying the peels on aluminium foil for approximately 2 hours in an oven that has been preheated to 75 °C (170 °F). Add the peels to the sugar after they have cooled.

Make sure that the spices or fruit peels are evenly distributed throughout the sugar. The whole, split vanilla bean or cinnamon stick can simply be inserted right into a container filled with sugar. Orange or lemon peels should be layered with sugar in your container. Seal the glass, affix a label and let it stand in a cool, dark place for one week.

Material

- **Castor sugar**
- **Spices**
- **Oranges or lemons**
- **Glass containers with screw top lids**
- **Leaves**
- **Glycerine from the pharmacy**
- **Brush**
- **Rubber bands**
- **Cling film**
- **Kitchen towels**
- **Raffia**

How to Make Aromatic Sugar

1 Cinnamon sugar: For 500 g (17 oz) sugar you will need 70 g (2.5 oz) cinnamon sticks. Cut the sticks lengthwise and distribute evenly in the sugar.

2 Vanilla sugar: You'll need 2–3 vanilla beans for 500 g (17 oz) sugar. Cut the beans lengthwise and stick them deep into the sugar.

3 Orange or lemon sugar: You will need peels from three oranges or four lemons for 500 g (17 oz) sugar. Layer the dried, cooled peels with the sugar in a glass container.

Decorate the Lid with Leaves

1 Clean a large, well-formed leaf and dry it carefully with a kitchen towel. Coat the top with plenty of glycerine. The leaf will absorb the glycerine and become more supple.

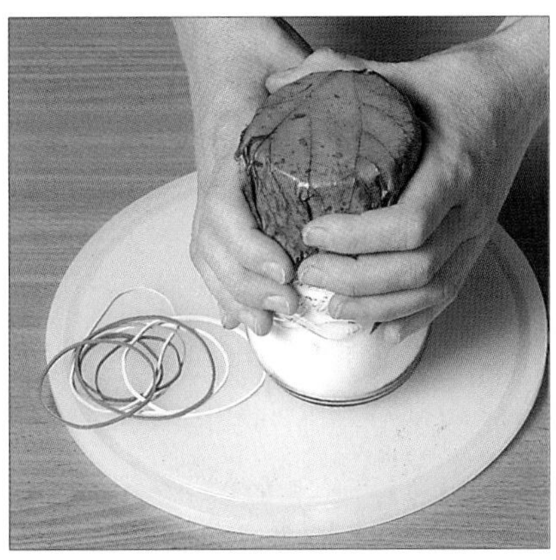

2 Lay the leaf over the screw top lid of the container, cover with cling film, press down, and secure with a rubber band. Let the glass stand in the refrigerator overnight.

3 Remove the cling film and carefully remove the surplus glycerine. Finally, gently wrap the leave with a piece of raffia.

You can simply mix noodles and mint pesto with fresh goat cheese for a simple and spicy meal. The savoury puff pastry bites are filled with pesto and make excellent appetisers.

Delicious Pesto to Give Away

Homemade herb pesto is always a welcome gift. Pesto is an ideal basis for a quick meal if you have invited friends for dinner and do not have a lot of time to cook.

The hectic pace of everyday life often doesn't allow a lot of time to prepare a large meal. However, you can still enjoy a delicious and healthy meal if you have pesto sauce on hand, because fresh pesto can be stored in the refrigerator for up to a week. With some noodles or rice, you can whip up a tasty meal in no time. For a tasty gift, you can fill decorative glass containers with screw top lids with the herb paste and affix a decorative label.

There are many ways to make pesto. Here are the ingredients for three delicious varieties:

(A) Basil-Arugula Pesto: 100 g (3.5 oz) pine nuts, one bunch basil and one bunch arugula, three garlic cloves, 125 g (4.5 oz) each Pecorino and Parmesan cheeses, salt and black pepper, approx. 1/4 l (9 fl oz) olive oil

(B) Mint Pesto: 100 g (3.5 oz) pine nuts, four garlic cloves, three bunches mint, juice of one lemon, salt, approx. 1/4 l (9 fl oz) olive oil, 200 g (7 oz) fresh goat cheese

(C) Olive-Pistachio Pesto: 60 g (2 oz) unsalted pistachio nuts, three garlic cloves, 1 tbsp green pepper, 250 g (9 oz) pitted green olives, 1 tbsp lemon juice, 175 g (6 oz) grated Parmesan cheese, salt, ca. 1/4 l (9 fl oz) olive oil

First roast the nuts or pine nuts in a pan. Place all the ingredients except the oil in a food processor and blend 10 to 15 seconds. (For the mint pesto, don't puree the cheese with the other ingredients, but add it separately.) Drizzle in the olive oil as you continue to mix the other ingredients until the pesto has a pasty texture Season with salt and pepper to taste. Fill a glass container with the pesto and drizzle with olive oil. Pesto freezes up to six weeks and keeps a week in the refrigerator.

Material

- **Nuts or pine nuts**
- **Herbs**
- **Garlic**
- **Lemons**
- **Olives**
- **Cheese**
- **Olive oil**
- **Spices**
- **Food processor**
- **Glass containers**

How to Prepare Pesto

1 Dry roast the pine nuts in a pan until they are light brown and have a fragrant aroma. Remove from the pan immediately as they burn easily.

2 Puree all the ingredients – except for the oil – in a food processor until the pesto has a creamy consistency.

How to Prepare Pesto with Pasta or Rice

1 Place cooked noodles in the pot. Stir in pesto and 1/8 litre (4 fl oz) of the water in which the noodles were cooked. Serve immediately.

2 You can also use the splendid pesto in a risotto. Simply stir 2–3 tbsp of pesto into cooked rice shortly before serving.

Puff Pastry Pinwheels as an Appetiser

1 Thaw 300 g (10 oz) puff pastry and lay it on a flat, floured work surface. Spread it with a thin layer of pesto (about 125 g/4.5 oz). Tightly roll both long sides to the middle.

2 Cut the double rolls in finger-thick slices and lay them rolled side down on a pan lined with parchment. Bake at 200 °C (390 °F) for 15–20 minutes (Do not overbake).

Wine bottles decorated with flowers are very beautiful and inviting. Secure the flowers or leaves with a piece of thick cording to match the greenery or the event.

Wine Bottles – Dressed Up for the Holidays

There are often greenery and flowers left over from large flower arrangements. Use these leftovers to create unusual decorated bottles.

A wine bottle decorated with flowers or greenery is a personal gift that you can even throw together at the last minute when you receive an invitation at short notice. For example, a small bouquet of flowers on a champagne bottle for a friend's thirtieth or fortieth birthday is always a welcome surprise. Or if you are hosting a large event with all the refinements, repeating your centrepieces in miniature on the various bottles is a real show stopper.

Apart from well-preserved greenery, which often outlasts ephemeral flowers in large flower arrangements, you can also use small sprigs, leaves, or shells to decorate the bottles.

It is relatively quick and easy to decorate a wine bottle; you only need an instinctive feel and some degree of dexterity, since a decoration like this is usually quite small. If you are inviting people over for a fancy dinner and want to decorate the various bottles with flowers, you don't have to decorate all the bottles beforehand. You can create one decoration such as the decoration to the right with the raffia ribbon, for example, which you can reuse as needed. When you open a new wine bottle, simply move the decoration to the next bottle, making sure that the label can still be read. Create the decoration to rest above the label and hang down next to it.

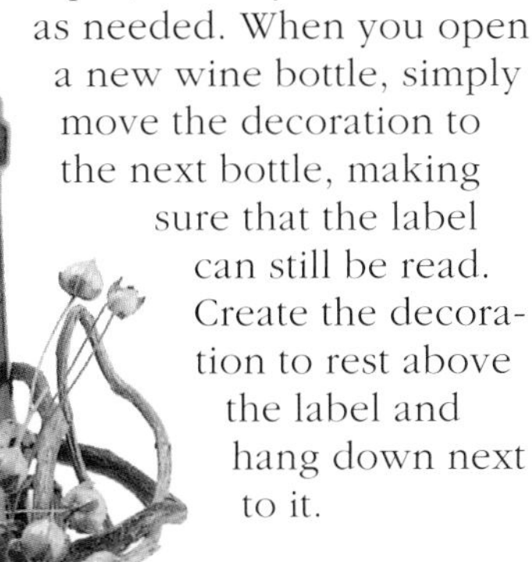

Material

- **Bottle**
- **Floral foam**
- **Greenery or flowers**
- **Ribbon**
- **Florist wire**
- **Raffia**
- **Glue or adhesive**
- **Scissors**

How to Decorate a Bottle Using Floral Foam

1 Cut a piece of floral foam and use the knife to cut it to form. Glue the foam to the bottle. If at all possible, the finished decoration should not cover the label of the bottle.

2 Insert some greens on the edges of the foam. Wrap a folded ribbon with wire and insert into the bottom of the foam. Glue one of the short edges to the top so the ribbon appears to go through the foam.

3 Insert some small flowers into the foam. If you want the decoration to be very festive, use larger, fuller flowers.

4 Carefully fill all the gaps with seed capsules or other greenery or plants. The decoration should be arranged quite densely, but should not look cluttered or overloaded.

How to Create a Simple Decoration with Raffia

1 Tie raffia around the neck of the bottle. Gather green leaves and some dried flowers together to create a small bouquet. Affix the stems to a ribbon with some glue.

2 Insert the bouquet behind the raffia and tighten it a bit so that the bouquet sits securely behind the ribbon. You can reuse this decoration on other bottles.

Take your places – dinner is served! Jot down the when and where on the menu so that the details tantalise the recipient at a glance. Gourmet cooks as well as motivated beginners will be thrilled to receive a set of spoons and cooking course accompanying the gift certificate.

Promising Gift Certificates

What at first glance looks like a small abstract work of art turns out upon closer examination to be a loving, handmade gift certificate for something thoughtful.

An invitation to a concert is concealed by a bunch of musical notes and a treble clef, the curtain rises on the stage to reveal an invitation to the opera, a roll of film promises an entertaining night at the cinema, and the table setting treats the recipient to a gourmet meal. These are ideal gifts for adventurous birthday boys and girls or sports fans who would be thrilled to receive gift certificates for activities such as tennis, golf, or fitness training.

To create a theatre stage, use a sharp knife to cut a slight gap in the middle of an ISO A4 piece of red card and fold it, then cut a 8 x 13 cm window in the middle of one of the halves. Glue a 4 x 21 cm strip of black paper under the window and the same amount of gold braid trim above it. Cut the mask medallion from a 5 x 7 cm piece of white card and glue it to the edge of the gold braid trim. Create the curtain from a gift ribbon 6 cm wide and 60 cm long. Cut the ribbon into four pieces of equal length and sew the sides of two pieces together to form two equal side panels. Make sure that there is no dust or lint on one of the open edges of pieces, gather the other piece together and glue the curtains to the back of the window. Secure it to the side with a 10-cm-long piece of cording. Tie a knot in the middle of a 10-cm-long piece of gold decorative ribbon, tie two more knots close to the edges about 7 cm from the middle knot, and glue it under the medallion. Fold a white ISO A5 card in the middle, cut off about 3 cm lengthwise, unfold and glue it behind the window.

Use two circles of paper and small paper rings on paper doilies (Ø 13 cm) for the place setting. Cut the silverware from a magazine.

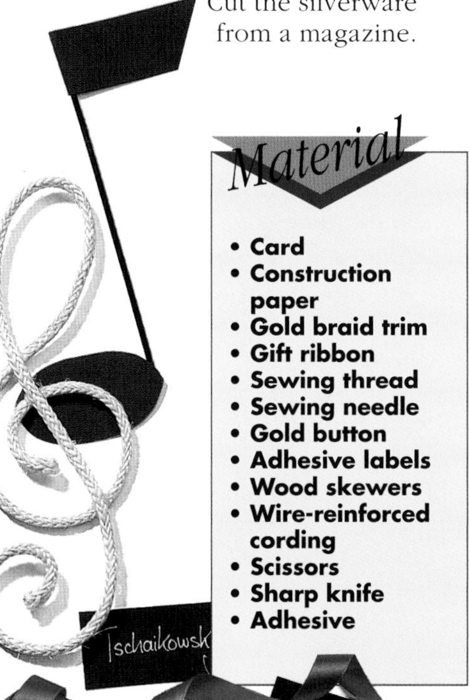

Material

- **Card**
- **Construction paper**
- **Gold braid trim**
- **Gift ribbon**
- **Sewing thread**
- **Sewing needle**
- **Gold button**
- **Adhesive labels**
- **Wood skewers**
- **Wire-reinforced cording**
- **Scissors**
- **Sharp knife**
- **Adhesive**

A Novel Theatre Ticket

1 You will need red and white card, gold braiding, black construction paper, decorative ribbon, a gold button, a sharp knife, black and gold felt-tipped markers, and red ribbon with gold trim, cut into four pieces.

2 Cut a window in the red card and glue on the black paper and gold braiding. Paint the medallion and sew the curtains from the red ribbon. Paint a pattern with the gold marker and gather the gold ribbon.

3 Frame the medallion with gold braiding and glue it above the curtains. Gather the curtains, glue them and secure them with cording. Glue the ribbon above the window.

CINEMA GIFT CERTIFICATE
Wrap foil around a film can. Cut strips of black construction paper, glue them together and affix small white labels along the edges.

How to Create a Gift Certificate for the Opera

1 Cut out three black circles and flags from a 5 x 9 cm piece of card for the notes. Bend wire in the shape of a treble clef and secure with glue where the wire overlaps.

2 Paint wood skewers black for the note stems and glue the circles and flags to them. Paint the treble clef gold and tie the notes to it with decorative ribbon.

How to Create a Hot Air Balloon

Tip

It takes some time and patience to master the technique of pressing and securing individually tailored ribbons into the pre-carved contours of the segments on the styrofoam ball, but the small balloon will look very similar to its real-life model once you do. If this method is too tricky you can always paint the balloon and pot instead of covering them with fabric.

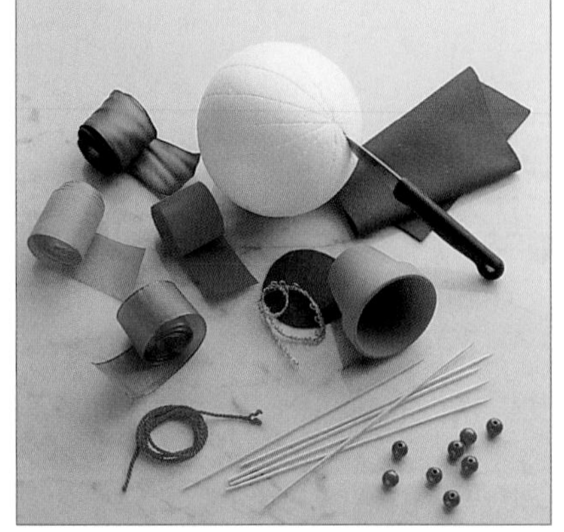

1 You'll need a small flower pot, felt, 4-cm-wide ribbons, pearls, wood skewers, cording, gold braid trim and a styrofoam ball (Ø 10 cm). Carve 16 segments into the ball with a knife.

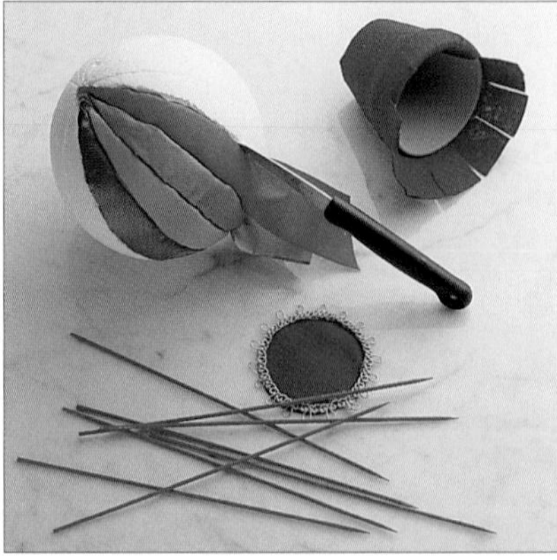

2 Press the ribbon into the grooves with a knife. Paint the skewers. Wrap the flower pot with felt. Cut a circle with a Ø of 6 cm from felt and glue gold braid to the edges.

3 Glue the skewers in the flower pot. Glue the felt circle to the top of the balloon. Affix pearls and cording to the balloon using straight pins. Glue the balloon to the wood skewers.

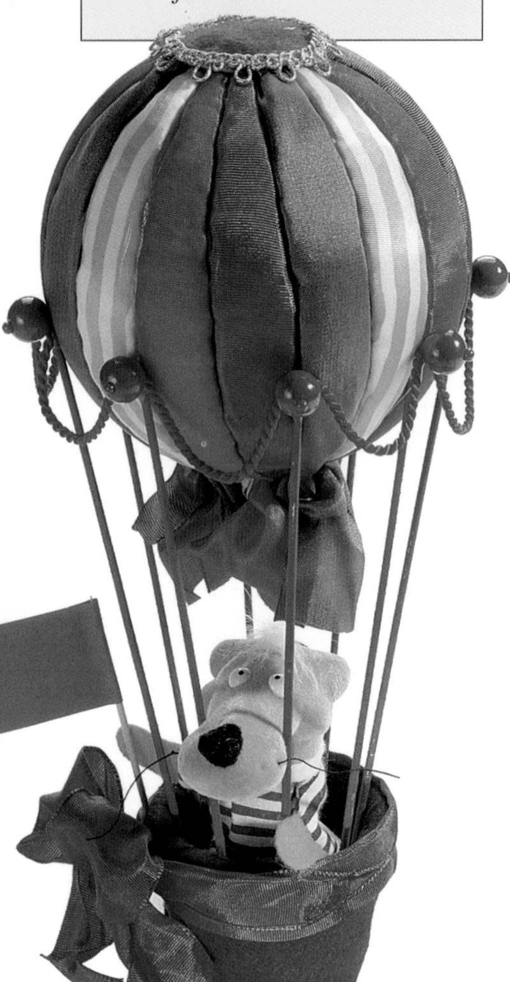

Idea

Use this variation to create a gift certificate fit for a fairy tale. In addition to the tiny suitcases, the small flying carpet contains a gift certificate for a plane trip. You can make the carpet yourself by sewing fringed braid trim to the edges of the wire-reinforced ribbon. The small boxes represent suitcases, and you can create a foam mattress by rolling up a small piece of foam rubber. A small piece of cardboard glued to the bottom of the carpet in the centre gives the flying carpet some stability.

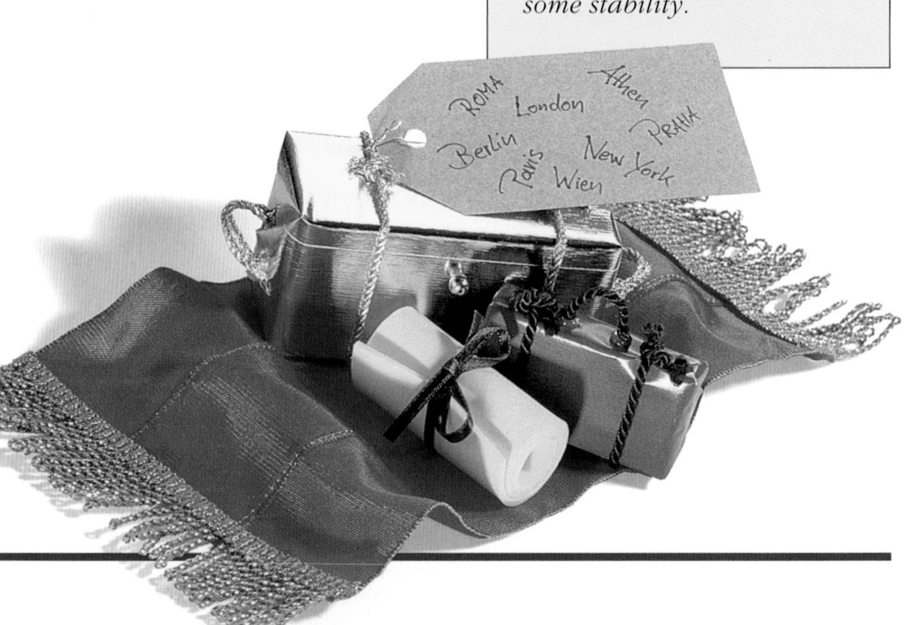

Unusual Gifts for Sports Fans

Learn how to create unique gift certificates for tennis fans or budding tennis players here: the fleece wrapping in the shape of a sweet is made of hand towels and contains real tennis balls. You can use the gift certificate to give the recipient tennis lessons or pay for a tennis court. Secure the ends of the towels by gathering them with bows of ribbon, fill them with tennis balls, and decorate them with tennis racquets and a label. You can also adapt this for golfers.

The yellow envelope contains a gift certificate for a fitness studio or for exercise clothes or equipment for fitness fans. The envelope is made of an ISO A4 piece of card, folded in half and closed with a matching triangle of corrugated card.

A cheeky detail for a fitness gift certificate is a striking measuring tape tied into a bow. The miniature barbells on the measuring tape bow may not make you stronger, but they can train your smile muscles. Even tennis or golf fans won't come up empty-handed.

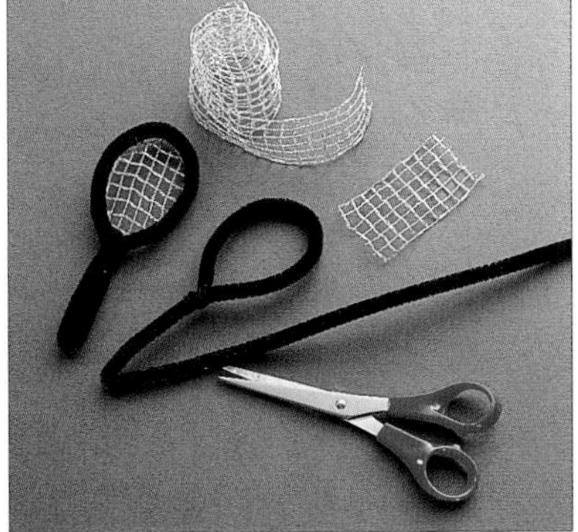

TENNIS RACQUET

Form the tennis racquets from an approx. 20-cm-long piece of pipe cleaner. First bend one end into a loop, then bend the other end up and hook it into the loop. Glue mesh ribbon to the back.

1 Fold an ISO A4 piece of card in half and close it with a triangle of corrugated card. Secure the measuring tape with a pipe cleaner, form several loops in the measuring tape and secure pairs of loops with the pipe cleaner.

2 Paint two different sized wooden wheels black to create the mini barbells. Glue a large and a small wheel to each end of a wood skewer painted silver. Tie a barbell onto each end of the pipe cleaner.

Rosemary, the typical herb used in Mediterranean cooking, gives herbal liqueur its hearty aroma. The herb dissolves easily in alcohol. Pour the finished liqueur into a decorative glass carafe. The sprig of rosemary in the bottle indicates what kind of liqueur it is.

Fine Liqueurs and Potent, Fruity Rum Pot

You can easily create these beautiful and delectable gifts yourself.

Ideas with a kick: rum pot and liqueurs add a refined touch to your desserts and are not very complicated to make. For example, black tea takes on an amazing aroma when sweetened with rum-flavoured rock sugar. When you need something quick, you can transform beverages into delicious drinks for surprise guests. Cappuccino liqueur is an excellent gift for Father's Day, for instance.

The freshness of summer fruit is traditionally preserved in rum pot – and who doesn't enjoy remembering the days of summer in the dead of winter?

Cappuccino liqueur may just arouse memories of your favourite vacation. You can find all the necessary ingredients for cappuccino liqueur in the step-by-step instructions to the right.

Egg liqueur (a.k.a. advocaat) is also cream-based. To make 1 litre (1 quart) spiced egg liqueur, beat 5 egg yolks, the mark of a vanilla bean and 150 g (5 oz) sugar with a hand mixer for 5 minutes until frothy. Add a pinch of powdered cinnamon and ground cloves, then fold a 340-ml (12-fl-oz) tin of condensed milk and 200 g (7 oz) cream into the egg mixture. Add 125 ml (4 fl oz) of brandy and blend well. Pour the liqueur into a clean bottle, seal it, and store in the refrigerator. It will keep for approximately two weeks.

To make 1 litre (1 quart) rosemary liqueur: rinse 2 sprigs fresh rosemary, shake dry, and insert it into a clean bottle. Brew 2–3 tbsp Earl Grey tea in 200 ml (7 oz) boiling water, let steep for 5 minutes, strain the tea leaves and stir 150 g (5 oz) honey into the tea. Add the tea to the rosemary and pour in 700 ml (25 fl oz) brandy. Allow the liqueur to steep for a week. If it is refrigerated it will keep for approximately six months.

Here's another tip: write the liqueur's best-before date on your homemade label. You may want to divide the liqueur between two smaller bottles.

Material

- **Sugar**
- **Vanilla bean**
- **Cream**
- **Instant espresso powder**
- **Sweetened cocoa**
- **Nutmeg**
- **Brandy**
- **Glass bottle**

How to Make Cappuccino Liqueur

1 Choose a suitable bottle or carafe for the liqueur. Wash it thoroughly with hot water, detergent, and a brush. Rinse it well with clear water.

2 Make a sugar syrup by dissolving 250 g (9 oz) sugar in 100 ml (3 fl oz) boiling water and letting it simmer for 10 minutes, stirring occasionally. Let the syrup cool.

3 Cut a vanilla bean lengthwise with a sharp knife and scrape out the tiny seeds. Stir the seeds and the whole vanilla bean into 300 g (10 oz) cream in a small saucepan.

4 Let the cream come to the boil and whisk in 2–3 tbsp instant espresso powder, 1–2 tbsp sweetened cocoa and a pinch of nutmeg. Fold in the warm sugar syrup.

5 Pour 250 ml (9 fl oz) brandy into the cream and blend thoroughly. Strain the mixture into a bowl through a fine sieve to remove the whole vanilla bean.

6 Pour the liqueur into the clean bottle. Close the bottle and store it in the refrigerator for a week to let it steep. The liqueur will keep four weeks in the refrigerator.

How to Preserve Summer Fruit in Rum Pot

1 Rinse and pat dry the fruit (300 g/ 10 oz of each kind) and remove stems, seeds and pits as needed. Cut larger fruit into bite-size pieces. Layer the fruit in a large container that can be sealed tightly.

2 Add sugar (half the weight of the fruit) to the fruit and stir in carefully. Let the fruit stand a bit to release some of its juice.

3 Pour in good quality rum to cover the fruit so it won't spoil. Seal and keep in a cool place. Add more fruit (with sugar and rum) as it comes into season. Shake or stir occasionally and top up as needed.

Idea

Rum pot is the best way to preserve the taste of summer fruit. Choose a rum with at least a 54% alcohol content, because it preserves the fruit better than one with a lower alcohol content. The preserved fruit is delightful with ice cream, tea, or champagne (as a cocktail). It is also a nice addition to gravy or wild game dishes, and will keep for months.

What goes into the rum pot when? Use only the freshest fruits!
June: strawberries (hulled), firm sweet cherries (pits and stems removed).
July: black currants, gooseberries (hulled), sour cherries (pits and stems removed).
August: apricots (stoned and halved), raspberries, peaches (peeled and quartered), plums (halved).
September: pears (peeled and sliced), seedless raisins.

Rum-Flavoured Rock Sugar

Tea lovers are not the only people who are cheered up by a strong cup of black tea on rainy weekends or gloomy winter days. Try serving your family and friends intoxicating rum-flavoured rock sugar at afternoon tea to warm them up.

First add the rum-flavoured rock sugar to the cups, then fill the cups with tea. The hot liquid will dissolve the rock sugar and impart a "liqueur-like" flavour and texture, sweetening the tea without substantially altering or covering up the drink's special characteristics.

Filled in beautiful glass containers, the rum-flavoured rock sugar is a novel gift idea that you can create in minutes. Dark rum is especially well-suited for this. Simply follow the directions below. You can affix a homemade label to the filled containers and decorate the label by gluing a few pieces of rock sugar to it. Give it as a gift along with some black tea in a small cellophane bag, which you can tie to the container with a colourful ribbon.

The aromatic rum-flavoured rock candy gives your table attractive flair in beautiful, decorative glass containers from a flea market or from a store. Serve it with tea along with crispy waffles or a fresh butter cake.

1 You can use all kinds of rock sugar (it can be white or brown, uncut or smooth) for this northern German specialty. You can also mix various types of rock sugar together.

2 Pour the rock sugar into a freshly washed glass container using a scoop. Make sure that you only fill the glass three-quarters of the way full so you have enough room for the rum.

3 Now fill the glass container with rum. Seal the container tightly and label it with a homemade label. The rum-flavoured rock candy can be stored and enjoyed almost indefinitely.

This is but one example of what your gift might look like. Fill a preserving jar and secure barbecue tongs to the jar with a ribbon. You can spice it up by adding chillies or hot peppers or fresh herbs and a label that contains a recipe. Perhaps you want to add the materials needed to get the flames going...

Spicy Ideas: Barbecue Sauce and Marinade

Cooking meat, fish, and vegetables over an open flame is an artform. These delicious grilled delicacies can be further improved with our homemade sauces.

There's nothing better than getting together in the summer for an outdoor picnic or barbecue. You can take the flavour of your food to the next level by serving it with savoury barbecue sauce and and exotic teriyaki sauce. Your guests are sure to love it. These sauces also make a great gift for a barbecue. Stored in attractive glass containers with lids or in beautiful bottles, they are a pleasure for the eyes as well as the palate.

Beautiful sealable bottles and glass containers are ideal for storing barbecue sauce and presenting it as a gift. Make sure the containers are dried thoroughly after you wash them, and be sure to prepare the sauces early enough to allow their aroma to fully develop. They will keep for two weeks in the refrigerator.

(A) Teriyaki marinade: 250 ml (9 fl oz) each dry sherry, oil and soy sauce; 6 garlic cloves; 6 tbsp sugar and 3 tbsp freshly grated ginger make about 750 ml (27 fl oz) of teriyaki sauce.

Mix all the ingredients in a bowl and marinate the food you want to grill in teriyaki sauce overnight.

(B) Barbecue sauce: 5 garlic cloves, 5 small onions, 500 ml (17 fl oz) tomato ketchup, 400 ml (14 fl oz) apple vinegar, 5 tbsp Worcester sauce and 5 tbsp brown sugar make ca. 1 litre (1 quart) of sauce.

Peel the onions and garlic. Press the garlic and finely chop it and the onions. Sauté them in oil for 10 minutes, add the other ingredients, and let simmer for 15 minutes. Because of the high sugar content, drizzle or brush the sauce over the food about 5–8 minutes before it is finished so that the sauce does not burn.

Material

- **Onions**
- **Garlic**
- **Tomato ketchup**
- **Apple vinegar**
- **Worcester sauce**
- **Brown and white sugar**
- **Sherry**
- **Oil**
- **Soy sauce**
- **Ginger root**
- **Nori seaweed**
- **Chopsticks**
- **Glass jars or bottles**
- **Fireplace matches**

How to Make a Teriyaki Marinade

1 Peel and finely grate the ginger root. Mix all the ingredients together in a bowl. Let the teriyaki sauce stand for about 1 hour.

2 Pour it into bottles. Wrap them with Nori seaweed (from Asian specialty stores) and secure chopsticks to the bottle with raffia.

How to Make Spicy Barbecue Sauce

1 Peel the onions and garlic. Crush the garlic with a large kitchen knife or garlic press and finely chop the onions and garlic. Sauté them in oil for about 10 minutes.

2 Add the rest of the ingredients, and simmer over low heat for about 15 minutes until the sauce thickens, stirring frequently. After the sauce has cooled, fill the bottles and store in the refrigerator.

DECORATIVE FIRE STARTERS
Roll up pieces of newspaper. Twist the ends in opposite directions and tie a knot in the middle. Decorate with ribbon or even some matches.

ORIGINAL PACKAGING
Place the glass jars filled with barbecue sauce in a small box with the fire starters and decorate with tomatoes or other vegetables.

You can trace a grape design that is fitting for a juice glass using silver glass paint outliner. If you are in a hurry, you can paint plates and drinking glasses made of blue glass freehand with stars and other geometric designs.

Hand-painted Glasses and Carafes

Glass painting has been a well-known art for centuries, and today you can admire valuable painted glass in museums. Here you can learn how to make these magnificent glasses yourself!

You can give simple glasses an aristocratic appearance using glass paint, glass paint outliner, and the templates in this book. Create beautiful works of art in minutes by adorning interesting glass objects with a fitting decoration. Romantic decorations are especially suited to classic glass forms, while simpler objects take on pizzazz with a functional design. But whatever you do, make sure that you don't wash hand-painted objects in the dishwasher!

Depending on the glass you select, you may have to enlarge or shrink the design on the template. The easiest way to do this is to use a photocopier. You may want to make several different sizes at the same time.

Insert the templates into the glass and trace the lines onto the glass using glass paint outliner. This comes in a range of colours and is available in tubes with nozzles at most craft stores. Keep a kitchen towel or cloth handy to clean the tip if it gets plugged. To create a straight line with outliner touch the tip onto the glass surface, then applying a gentle, even pressure, lift the nozzle away from the surface and stretch the outliner along in a straight line. Touch the nozzle down on the glass surface at the end of your line. If you make a mistake or don't like the design, simply let the outliner dry and scrape it off with a razor blade. Once the outliner has dried fill in the areas between the outlines with glass paint. Set the colour by baking the pieces in the oven, following the manufacturer's instructions.

Material

- **Glasses and carafes**
- **Gold & silver glass paint outliner**
- **Glass paint**
- **Small paintbrush**
- **Scissors**
- **Adhesive tape**
- **Terry cloth towel**
- **Kitchen towels**
- **Batting**
- **Templates on pages 56–57**

1 Make different-sized copies of the template you have chosen and cut it out close to the design. Insert the template into the glass, bending it as necessary.

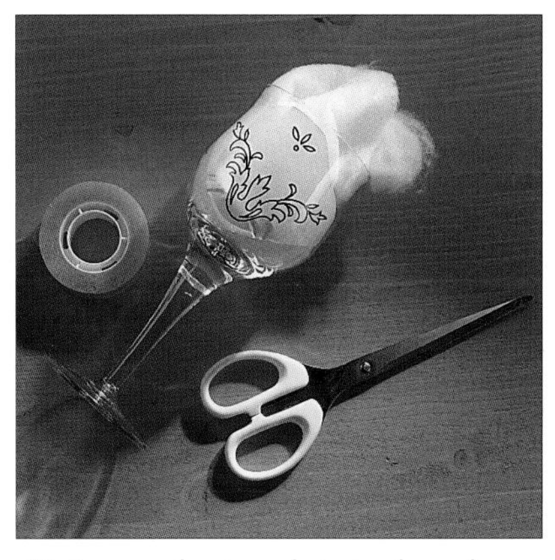

2 Secure the template to the edge of the glass with tape. Push a piece of batting into the glass, which will ensure that the paper with the design nestles against the glass and does not slip.

3 Lay a terry cloth towel onto the working surface and position the glass so that it cannot roll off. Brace your arms and trace the outer edges with the glass paint outliner.

4 Copy the design for the foot of the glass and trace it onto the glass. Fill in all design surfaces with glass paint and let dry overnight, then fire it in your oven according to the manufacturer's instructions.

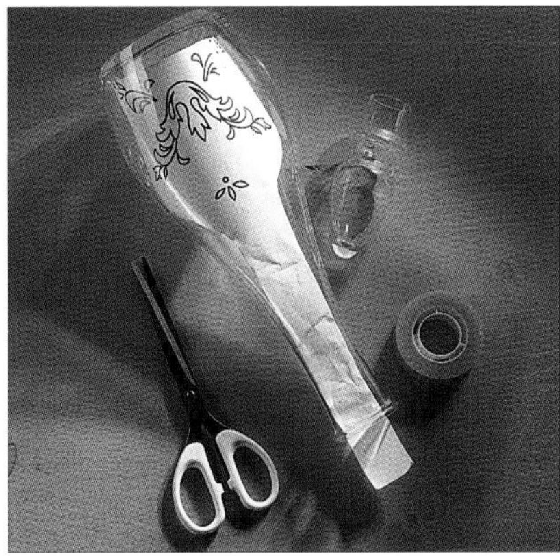

5 Copy the carafe design and cut it close to the edge, leaving a long strip in the centre. Roll the template and insert it into the bottle. Secure the paper to the upper rim of the bottle.

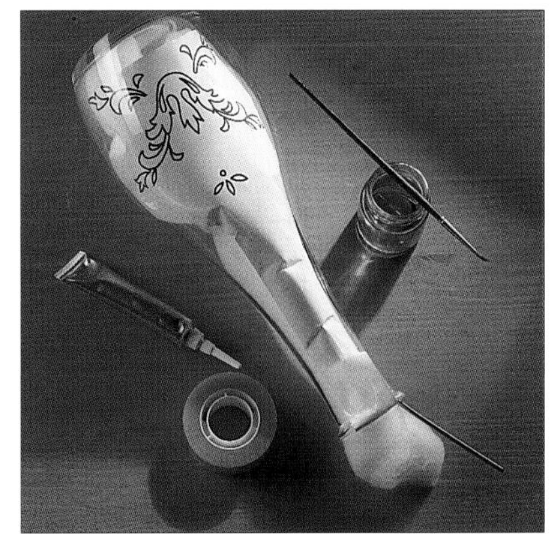

6 Cut out a piece of batting and use a long knitting needle to insert it into the bottle behind the paper so that the design is nestled against the glass, then paint it and fire it in the oven.

Try decoratong a large bunch of **Buxus sempervirens** *with useful tools for a DIY enthusiast. Or present someone who has wanderlust with a compass on a tray that is decorated with exotic greenery and grasses.*

The Gift of Flowers

Have you ever been invited somewhere and needed a gift? If you know the host's hobby, you can create a bouquet of flowers and integrate implements that relate to their hobby.

You can arrange almost any objects that are about the same size as a bouquet of flowers or a flower arrangement. For example, all kinds of kitchen utensils for a cooking enthusiast, or brushes and pliers for a DIY enthusiast. People with a sweet tooth are thrilled to receive sweets and gourmets could find an invitation to a French restaurant between the flowers. Other original ideas include tucking lottery tickets or banknotes into the bouquet.

Your first decision is whether you want to give your recipient a bouquet of flowers or a floral arrangement. If you want to give a floral arrangement, keep in mind that you will also be giving them the container. But the size and weight of the gifts also play a role. You can tie lighter objects together with wire and tie them to the arrangement, while heavier objects will be better supported with a piece of floral foam. In any case, make sure the arrangement is stable enough that it can be easily transported.

Large containers such as a baking form for avid bakers do not have to be completely filled. Simply cover some of the tin with moss and arrange one or two small objects around it.

You may include a few tips for the care of the plants: to enjoy the arrangement as long as possible, do not place it near a heater, add water every day and spray the moss with water often to keep it moist. Flowers will stay fresh longer if you add a floral preservative to the water and only replace the water absorbed by the flowers. Bouquets that contain gifts should not be untied immediately, since they will fall apart.

Material

- **Baking ring**
- **Floral foam**
- **Moss**
- **Flowers**
- **Flowering greens**
- **Wire (optional)**
- **Pot of chives**
- **Jalapeno peppers**
- **Kitchen utensils**
- **Knife**
- **Watering can**

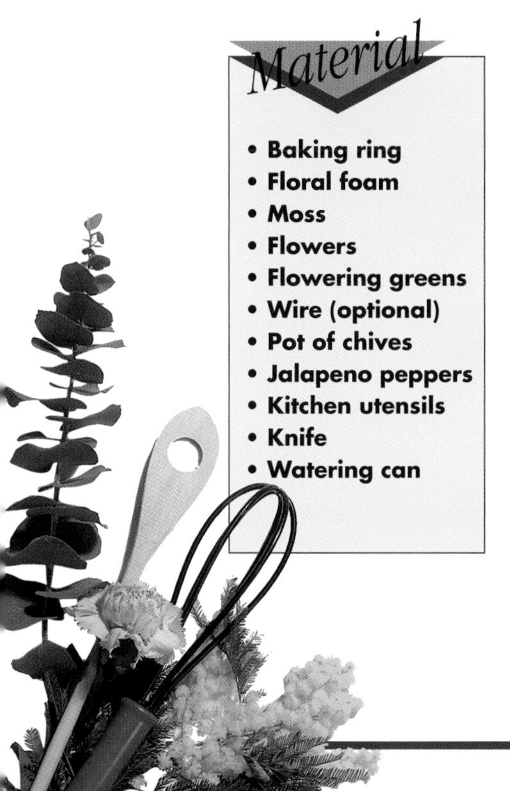

How to Create a Floral Arrangement with Kitchen Utensils

1 Lay three large pieces of floral foam side by side. Position a ring-shaped baking pan on top and use a knife to trace around the outside and inside opening of the pan.

2 Cut the floral foam about one centimetre smaller than the baking pan. Round off the bottom edges so that the foam fits into the cake pan. Place the foam in the pan and water it thoroughly.

3 Place a pot of chives (the pot should be slightly larger than the opening in the centre of the ring) on top of the pan. Soak the moss briefly in warm water so it looks fresh then cover the front half of the pan with it.

4 Arrange longer items such as eucalyptus branches, rubber spatulas and mixing spoons in the rear half of the pan. Bind the utensils together with wire or anchor them directly to the floral foam.

5 Fill out the arrangement with purple sea lavender, yellow mimosas, pink carnations or other flowers. Those in front should be somewhat smaller than those in back.

6 To give the arrangement a finishing touch, add some jalapeno peppers and smaller blossoms in the front part of the baking pan, close to the pot of chives.

An Original Gift for a Hobby Gardener

1 One package of cat grass will cover 25 cm of surface in balcony planters. Position the cat grass container in a planter and fill the remaining space with floral foam. Sow the grass seeds and water daily.

2 After a week or so the grass will be approx. 10–15 cm high. Insert small daisies between the blades of grass so that their blossoms just peek over grass.

3 Arrange small gardening implements like a trowel or gardening shears in the floral foam. Secure bags of seeds with wire and let them hang over the edges of the planter.

Tip

If you do not have enough time to grow cat grass you can always give someone a bouquet that contains packets of plant seeds. All you need is some attractive grass and greenery from a flower shop as well as a few packets of seeds. Glue a long piece of wire to the back of the seed packets and gather the plants and packets into a bouquet. Your gift will be complete when you finish it off with a large, green bow.

A Bouquet of Flowers and Beauty

Give a woman everything she needs to be beautiful: bottles of perfume, small bars of soap, make-up brushes, and make-up. Together with a Calla lily and some greenery, you can tie everything together to create a noble bouquet. To provide a truly regal touch, you can wrap the bouquet with a wide collar of tissue paper to match the colour of the lily.

You can buy Calla lilies year round, but not every florist carries them. You can replace the Calla lily with another striking flower, such as a blazing red anthurium, a Bird of Paradise flower or a Gerber daisy.

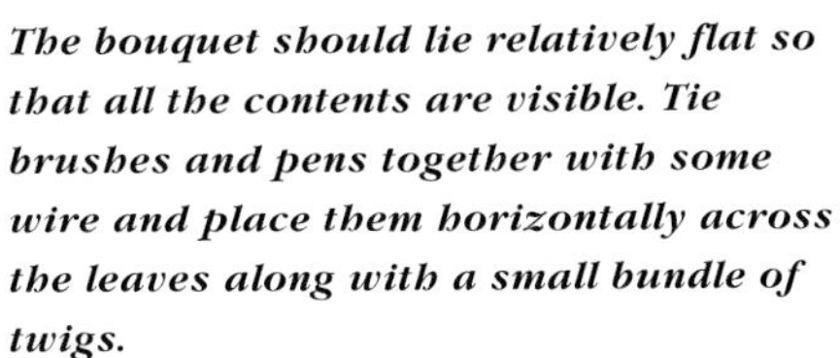

The bouquet should lie relatively flat so that all the contents are visible. Tie brushes and pens together with some wire and place them horizontally across the leaves along with a small bundle of twigs.

1 Create the middle of the bouquet first. Start with the Calla lily and two green branches. Wrap the bundled stems with wire, which you can extend downward to use as a stem.

2 Start securing the cosmetic items to the bouquet with wire, alternating them with greenery to make a bouquet, making sure the Calla lily always remains in the centre.

3 Fold a large piece of wrapping tissue in half to make a narrow strip. Wrap the tissue around the bouquet with the folded edge facing out to form a collar. Tape or glue the sides of the paper together.

A gift basket is the ideal last-minute gift. Decorate a medium-sized wicker basket with flowers and fill it with wine, good cheese, and fruit. You can select flowers that match the form and style of the basket.

An Attractive Gift Basket with Flowers

Do you still need a good gift idea? A gift basket filled with delicacies like the one above is a welcome gift for many occasions.

A ready-made gift basket is not often very reasonably priced. You can save the money for the decorative design by putting together the basket yourself. Wicker baskets with handles or even wooden crates are perfectly suitable for this. You can coordinate the flowers and the various delicacies to match the season or the occasion. A gourmet basket is a delicious and practical table decoration that you can use to present your host with a truly tasteful array of fruits, sweets or alcoholic beverages and spirits.

Let the shape of the basket inspire you when planning how to decorate it. For example, you might decorate the rim of a round basket with a garland of flowers. Secure the flowers together with a piece of twine, which will make the garland extremely flexible and let you shape it in any direction. Depending on the shape of the basket, you can attach the flowers in different locations on the sides or outside on the rim of the basket. You can secure a shorter garland to the handle. Affix it to the side of the handle so the decorations are not damaged when the basket is carried.

To create a bouquet, carefully tie the flowers below the blossoms with floral wire so that they are as stable and compact as possible. Use winding wire for extra strength to secure the bouquet to the basket. Bend it in the middle to shape it like a hair pin, position the flowers inside the bend and stick the ends of the wire through the basket. Twist the ends together inside the basket and stick them back through the basket to secure it.

Material

- **Basket**
- **Plants**
- **Winding wire**
- **Florist wire**
- **Floral crepe**
- **Thin twine**
- **Cotton batting**
- **Raffia**
- **Silk ribbon for bows**
- **Scissors**

How to Tie and Secure a Garland of Flowers

1 Tie a knot in the end of a piece of string or twine. Attach the florist wire below the knot, using it to secure flowers to the string and twist the ends to form a garland.

2 Attach winding wire to the garland, insert the ends through the basket, and twist the ends together a few times inside the basket.

How to Tie and Secure a Bouquet of Flowers

1 Gather the plants together to make a bouquet. Position moist batting between the stems and wrap the batting with floral crepe.

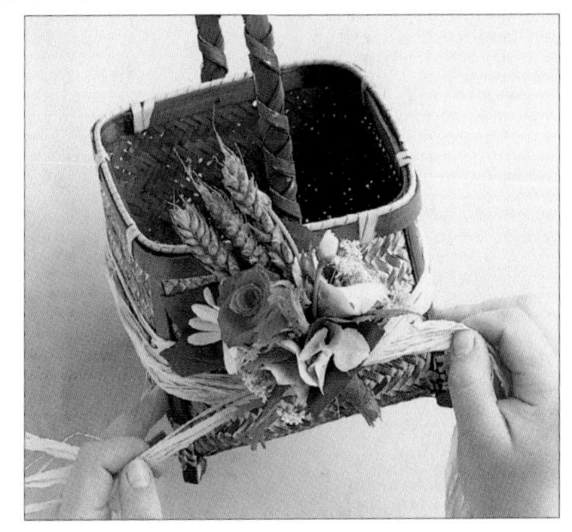

2 Tie the bouquet of flowers to the basket by tying it to the basket several times with raffia. Tie additional rafia around the basket and bouquet for decoration.

How to Decorate a Handle with Flowers

1 Attach the florist wire at the bottom of the handle. Tie flowers on the handle closely spaced, with the blooms facing downward, so that the handle is covered with flowers.

2 Create a bouquet as described above and secure it to the handle with wrapping wire. You can even tie a matching silk ribbon around the bouquet.

So that you always know which herbs are which, it's helpful to label each pot with a little sign. Write the name of the herb on a colourful piece of card and affix it to a plant marker. If possible, each herb should get its own colour.

Lovely Pots for Kitchen Herbs

Fresh herbs are not only great additions to any recipe, but they also look nice. Unfortunately they are often stuck in boring pots. With a little colour, raffia or twine, you can have a unique pot for your herbs.

Fancy, ornately decorated flowerpots are often extremely expensive. With just a little effort and affordable materials you can transform simple plastic or clay pots into decorative showstoppers.

You might as well create an entire herb garden! Fresh herbs not only grow well on a sunny kitchen windowsill, but they are also a real eye-catcher. And you can snip off a few leaves whenever you need them.

You can decorate used pots as well as new ones. If you are careful, you will not even have to re-pot herbs that have already been planted. Before you begin painting them, the pots should be washed with detergent to remove any dust particles or traces of grease. The paint will adhere better and not peal off as easily.

Use your imagination to come up with a design. Simple geometric shapes are a good choice – as are stylish plant designs. You can mix paint colours yourself to create more unusual shades.

When wrapping the pot with twine, make sure that the rows are smooth and close together. The surface of the pot should not show through the rows. You can glue the beginning and end of the twine to the pot or tie it into a thick, visible knot.

You can buy the necessary materials such as brushes, decorative paint, raffia, adhesive and twine in any craft store.

How to Decorate a Flowerpot with Paint and Raffia

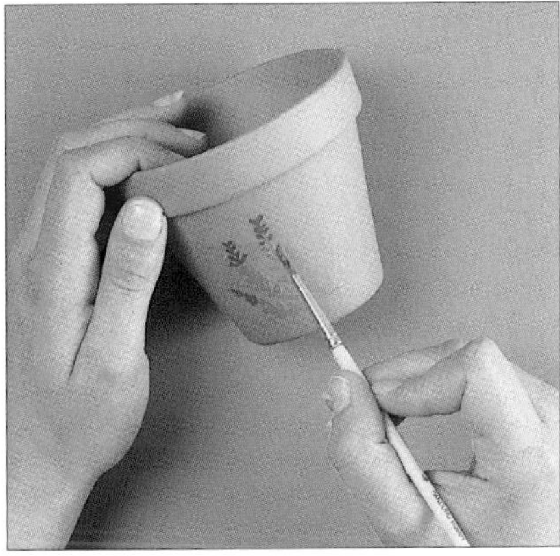

1 Draw the design onto the pot in pencil. Apply the bottom layer of paint (here it is green) and then apply the various colours for the design.

2 Let the paint dry. Wrap the rim of the pot several times with raffia. Tie the ends of the raffia to form a large knot.

How to Decorate a Flowerpot with Twine

1 Apply a thin, even coat of adhesive to the surface that will be wrapped with twine.

2 Start the first row of twine directly below the rim of the pot and wrap the twine continuously around the pot. The rows should be close together.

Material

- **Flowerpots**
- **Decorative paint**
- **Paint brushes**
- **Raffia**
- **Adhesive**
- **Twine**
- **Scissors**
- **Pencil to draw the design**

This is also a great idea to make sure that tips and tricks from grandmother's kitchen are not forgotten. You can decorate your recipe file folder in various ways depending on the fabric, ribbon and the colour of the cardboard. Combine ecru-coloured linen and a rustic ribbon or blue corduroy and a striped ribbon for a personalised look.

A Personalised Recipe File for Hobby Chefs

Are you one of those people who loves to try out new recipes? Write down your favourite recipes in a small portfolio and give it to someone as a gift.

A collection of your secret or favourite recipes is also a practical idea for your own kitchen. Create a portfolio out of cardstock and cover the front with fabric – preferably one that matches the contents. Create divider pages for meat and poultry dishes, vegetables, salads, bread, sweets and any other category that suits you to organise your recipes and help you find them quickly. You can hold the pages together with a beautiful ribbon.

The recipe file folder is created using approx. 1-mm-thick card, then covered with fabric.

First use the templates on pages 58–61 to cut out two equal rectangles and a narrow strip from the card and two pieces of fabric. Place the fabric right side down and position the rectangles next to each other in the centre of the fabric. Run a bead of glue around the edge of the card, pull the fabric over the edges of the card, and glue the fabric to the card. Do not glue the card directly to the fabric, since the glue might seep through and mar the appearance. Then glue the smaller piece of fabric to the inside the same way to completely cover the card.

Prepare the divider pages using colourful pieces of card. You can identify each section with symbols. Punch holes in the pages, centre them inside the folder, transfer the hole positions to the fabric and create eyelets based on the markings. Punch holes in the recipe pages, position the recipe pages and index pages in the file, thread a ribbon through the eyelets and pages, and tie a pretty bow inside or outside the file.

Material

- **Card, approx. 1 mm thick**
- **Fabric**
- **Textile glue**
- **Pencil**
- **Scissors or knife**
- **Pinking shears**
- **Hole punch**
- **Eyelets and eyelet tool**
- **Decorative ribbon**
- **Colourful card**
- **Gold marker**
- **Black felt-tipped marker**
- **Templates on pages 58–61**

1 Cut out three pieces of card and two pieces of fabric according to the templates. Position the card next to each other on the wrong side of the larger piece of fabric, leaving a border of approx. 5 mm.

2 Fold the corners of the material over the card and glue them. Run a bead of glue around the perimeter of the card, pull the fabric over its edges and glue it to the card. Make sure the fabric is even and taut.

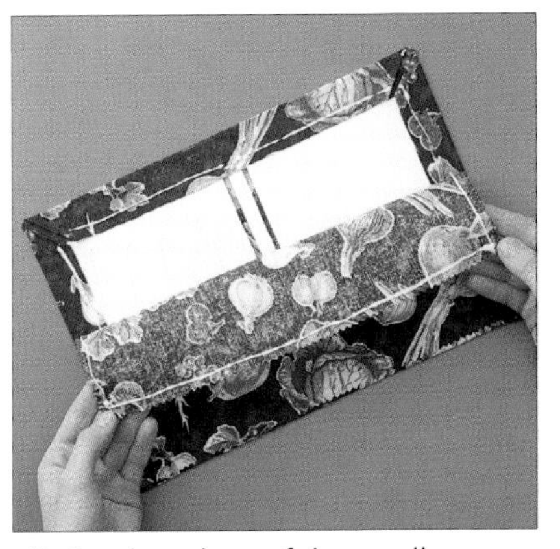

3 Cut the edges of the smaller piece of material with pinking shears and use it to cover the inside of the card. To cover the card, apply a thin layer of glue to the card and the outer edges of the material.

4 Cut out dividers from colourful card and punch holes in them. Divide recipes into sections and cut out enough tabs. Draw symbols from the templates on the tabs with gold marker. Outline the edges in black.

5 Position a divider in the folder on the right side and transfer the position of the holes with a felt-tipped pen. Punch holes through the cardboard and fabric based on the markings and attach eyelets.

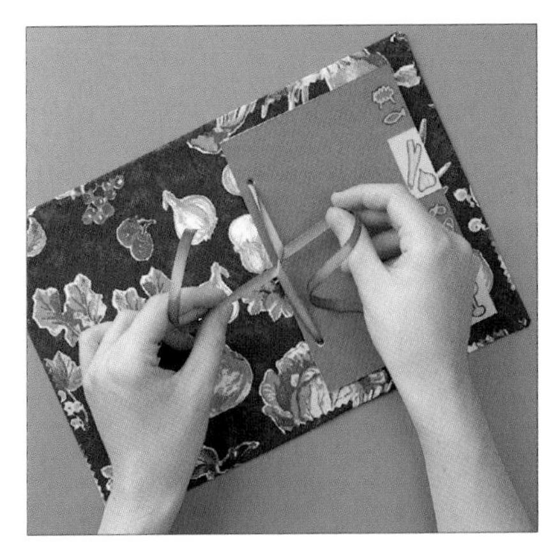

6 Thread a ribbon through the eyelets and last divider. Punch holes in the recipe pages and arrange them according to the same principle. Tie a bow to the inside or outside of the folder.

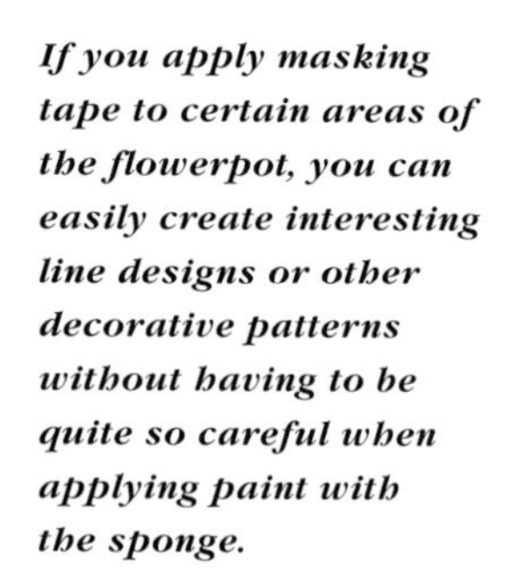

If you apply masking tape to certain areas of the flowerpot, you can easily create interesting line designs or other decorative patterns without having to be quite so careful when applying paint with the sponge.

Sponge Painting on Flowerpots

You can transform simple terra cotta flowerpots into beautiful works of art using nothing more than opaque paint, masking tape and a sponge.

You can never have enough of these flowerpots – in all shapes and colours. Using the sponging method, they lose their everyday appearance and look so interesting that you might just put them on a shelf for decoration. First paint the outside of the pot in a base colour with acrylic or latex paint, then mix a lighter and darker tone of the same basic colour. Gently apply both colours onto the dried base colour with a natural sponge, being careful not to use too much paint.

You can paint old or new flowerpots using this technique. You just have to make sure that the pots are completely clean and dry, otherwise the paint will not adhere correctly. You can use a regular household sponge, but you will get even better results if you use a natural sponge. It may cost a bit more, but it also lasts longer. Wash the sponge thoroughly with soap and water after each use.

Base colours are available in all imaginable hues, but it is often cheaper and even more interesting to mix the desired shade yourself. In this case, buy a base colour, such as medium blue, that you can mix with white and black to get the tones you want. This way you can be sure that the colours will be a good match.

It is important that the base colour dry completely before you apply the tape, because if it is not dry you will pull up the colour when you remove the tape. Always remove the strips of tape slowly and carefully.

If you want to keep the terra cotta colour of the flowerpot as your base colour or if the pot is already painted, you can save yourself the trouble of painting a base coat and just start decorating.

- **Flowerpot**
- **Opaque paint**
- **Clear varnish**
- **Sponge**
- **Paint brushes**
- **Masking tape**
- **Pencil**
- **Ruler**

Create Stripes Using the Sponge Technique

1 Pour some opaque paint onto a plate for the base colour. Dip the sponge in the paint and gently apply it to the surface of the flowerpot. Continue until the entire surface is covered. Let the paint dry.

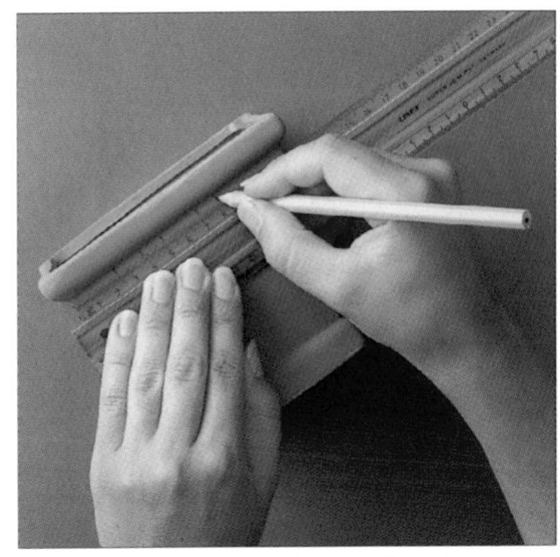

2 Decide on the design for the flowerpot and use a ruler to measure where the lines will go. Trace light marks onto the pot with a pencil where you would like the lines to be.

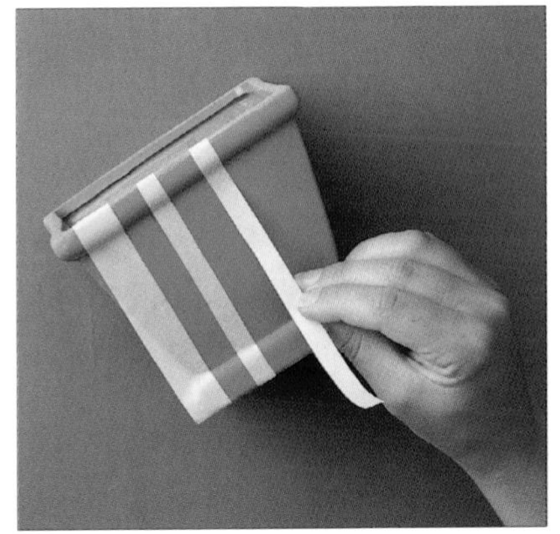

3 You may have to cut the tape into smaller strips depending on the desired design. Apply the tape so that the areas that should not be painted are completely covered.

4 Mix a lighter and darker tone using the base colour. Apply the darker colour to the flowerpot first until all the unmasked areas are covered and you are satisfied with the way it looks. Let it dry.

5 Apply the lighter colour over the darker colour until the pot looks like you imagined. Let this side dry and continue this process until all sides are finished.

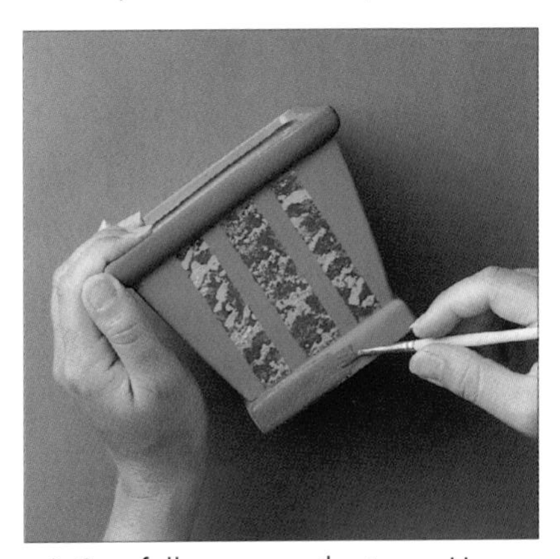

6 Carefully remove the tape. Use a small paint brush to paint the bottom and top rims of the pot with the darker colour so that it looks more polished. Let the paint dry.

The Freehand Sponging Technique

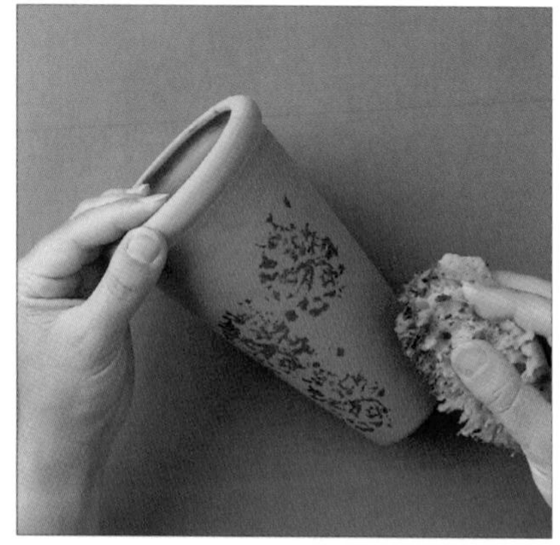

1 Dip the sponge in the base colour and apply the paint to the entire surface of the flowerpot. Let the paint dry. Mix lighter and darker tones. Apply the darker paint to the entire surface of the pot and let dry.

2 Then apply the lighter paint to certain areas of the surface using the sponge. Distribute the paint decoratively onto the surface. You can reapply the darker colour to the edge of the pot.

Tip

The design doesn't have to use straight lines. You can apply the tape diagonally and sideways and create beautiful designs this way. A witty variation is to rip off small pieces of tape, apply them haphazardly to the pot and then paint over them. When you finally remove the tape, you will find you've created a unique design.

Idea

All you need to create original flowerpots, beside paints and a sponge, is a little imagination. For example, you can select warm colours that remind you of an autumn morning in the forest. First apply the base colour and then use a sponge to apply many different colours at the same time. Experiment with various techniques by applying the paint to the pot using the entire surface of the sponge or just the edge.

Paint On Beautiful Stars

You can create an easy and unique design by decorating an object with small, self-adhesive stars or other similar motifs. You can buy the stars in paper goods or craft stores. Simply apply the stars as you would tape and cover areas that should not be painted. When you remove the stars, the design will appear in the base colour on the pot. If needed, you can use a needle to remove the stars.

You can also create your own designs and cut them from self-adhesive labels. Let your imagination run wild! Cut out as many designs as you need. You can do this freehand and create shapes that vary somewhat from one another or you can trace them with a template so that they are all uniform. Cut out the shapes with scissors or a knife, with a mat or some sort of underlay underneath. Affix them onto the pot at regular or varied intervals.

A terra cotta pot that you have transformed using colour and decorations can still be used as a flowerpot, but you can also use it to hold pens on your desk or as an eye-catching dash of colour on a shelf.

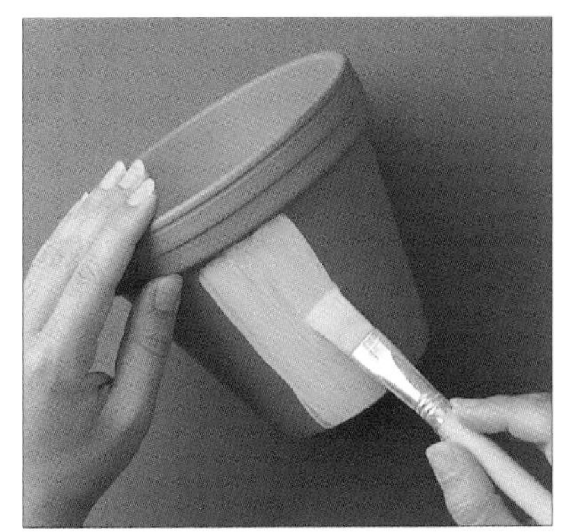

1 Paint the flowerpot, including the rim, in a base colour using a wide brush or a sponge. Let the paint dry.

2 Apply the self-adhesive stars at regular intervals over the entire pot. Alternate large and small stars so it looks more lively.

3 Paint over the base colour and the stars using a different colour. Let the paint dry and then carefully remove the stars. Seal the pot with clear varnish.

An egg that you have wrapped in soft lamb's ear leaves is a unique decoration, because it has a very fleecy surface. You can also wrap egg halves made of cardboard in beech leaves and fill them with delectable sweets.

Stylish Easter Eggs with Leaf Wraps

Hide Easter sweets in a unique way – if you wrap traditional Easter eggs made of pasteboard or cardboard in green leaves, the eggs will look very natural and sophisticated at the same time.

Several types of leaves are suitable for wrapping the eggs: you can use green ivy leaves or dried beech leaves in striking colours that you collected in the autumn. To use the eggs as decoration, arrange them on leaves lining a plate or a basket. Decorated with a festive ribbon, these eggs are the perfect packaging for an Easter gift. Used as a classic Easter egg, filled with fancy sweets, they make great small gifts.

Easter eggs become tiny works of art when they are wrapped with overlapping leaves. The paper eggs shown here can be bought in craft stores, but any other decorative egg can also use be used for this.

If the eggs are solely for decoration, you should glue the two sides together before you begin. If you want to fill the eggs with sweets or use them as packaging you should wrap the individual halves and then put them together after they have dried.

Fresh ivy leaves as well as dried greenery, such as beech leaves, are especially well suited for this. To dry them, lay the leaves inside a newspaper and press until they are uniformly flat. If you dry them on only one surface, the edges of the leaves will curl and you will not be able to press them flat. To help the leaves lie flat against the surface of the egg, you can wrap them with a gauze bandage after you glue them down. Carefully remove the bandage only after the glue has dried. You should then spray the egg with matte or glossy acrylic sealer. One product especially well suited for this is floral sealer, available at florists and craft stores.

Material

- **Leaves**
- **Cardboard Easter eggs**
- **Adhesive tape**
- **Wood glue or wallpaper paste**
- **Organza ribbon**
- **Scissors**
- **Clear varnish**

How to Wrap a Decorative Egg with Leaves

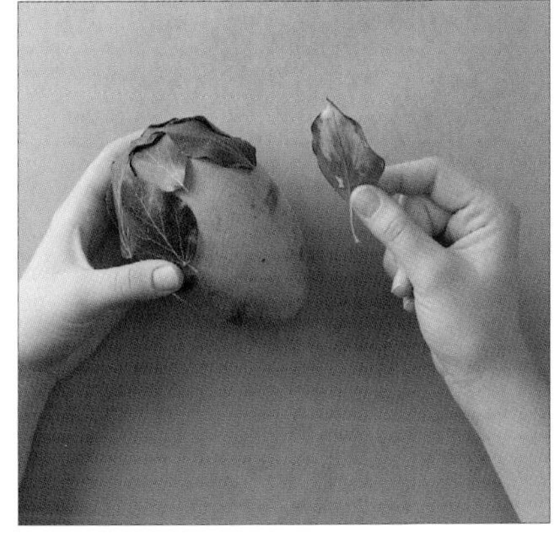

1 Glue the two halves of the eggs together. Apply a thin layer of wood glue to the back of the leaves and glue them to the eggs with the tips pointing the same direction. Start at the blunt end of the egg.

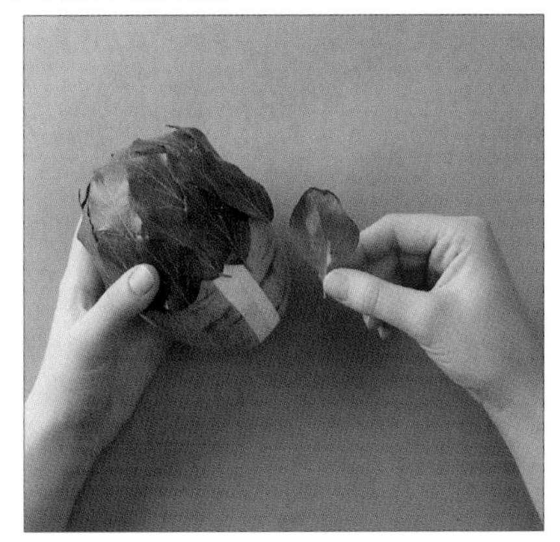

2 Cover the egg completely in uniform rows, making sure the rows of leaves slightly overlap one another. Glue all the leaves with their tips pointing in the same direction.

3 Press the leaves firmly to the egg with the palm of your hand. Glue a leaf to the spot where the leaves all meet on the blunt end of the egg.

4 Tie an organza ribbon around the egg, letting the ends dangle. Tie several loops to secure the loose ends of the ribbon.

How to Wrap Individual Egg Halves with Leaves

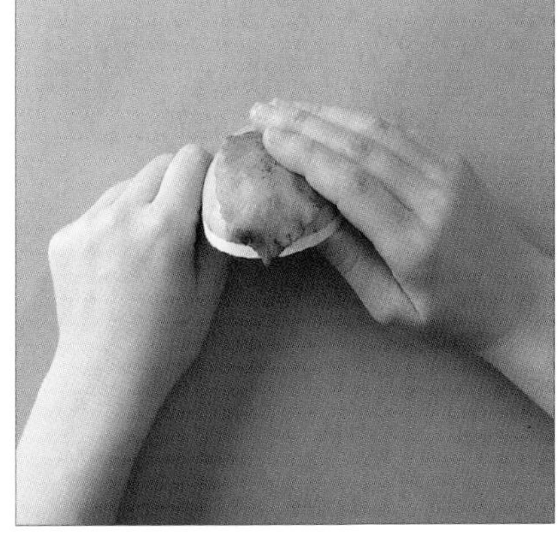

1 Glue each of the halves separately. Begin by gluing the first leaf onto the egg with the tip pointing toward the pointed end of the egg. Let the glue dry a bit.

2 Glue the next leaves over the previous ones so that they overlap and fold them over the top of the egg. Spray the eggs with varnish so that they glisten.

The scent of these glass candles, which are scented with the peels of oranges, lemons, and cumquats, have a refreshing effect. Gilded walnut halves are unique and thoughtful little gifts. Be sure to hold the wicks securely when pouring the wax and wait until the wax has cooled to let go so that they don't sink into the candle.

Christmas-scented Candles

When Advent comes around and the scent of vanilla, gingerbread, and almonds from baking cookies fills the air you know that Christmas is not far away.

The traditional spices used in Christmas cookies, such as cinnamon, star anise and cloves, used to be very expensive because the routes from the Orient, from where they were imported, were long and difficult. Today you can buy them in every supermarket.

You can also circulate their delicate fragrance another way: by adding the spices to candle wax. Every room will be filled with the fragrance created by the rising warmth of the burning candles.

You can buy granulated wax in ready-to-melt mixtures in any craft store. If you have candles left over from last Christmas that are almost burned down, you can use these as well. Break up the candle carefully with a knife, remove the wick, and melt down the wax.

There are many different types of candle wicks available and each has a specific application and a specific amount of fuel it is capable of consuming. You should keep the approximate circumference of the jars you plan to use for the candles in mind when buying the wicks.

You can buy dried orange or lemon slices in craft stores, but they are also very easy to make yourself. Cut the fruit into approximately 1-cm-thick slices and hang them over a heat source or radiator with some string or twine. The slices will dry out completely in about a week. You can also use an oven or microwave if you need it to go quicker.

To remove the candles from the jars, hold the glass under hot running water and carefully pull on the cinnamon stick or dowel tied to the wick.

Material

- **Granulated wax**
- **Candle wicks**
- **Glass jars or glasses**
- **Star anise**
- **Cinnamon sticks**
- **Bay leaves**
- **Cloves**
- **Dried citrus slices**

How to Pour Candles with Spices

1 Melt the granulated wax in a small saucepan over medium heat. A marmalade jar or water glass are especially good moulds for the candle. Pour about 2 cm of melted wax into the glass.

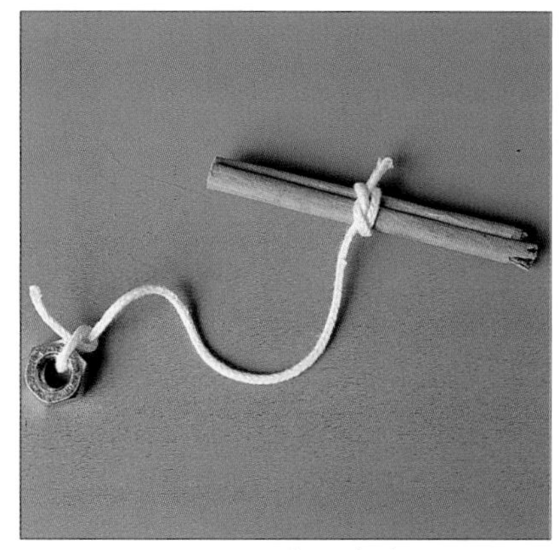

2 Cut a section of wick that is about 15 cm longer than the length of your mould. Attach a small weight to one end of the wick and wrap the other end around a cinnamon stick or dowel and tie a knot.

3 Press the wick and the cinnamon sticks into the soft wax. Lay the cinnamon stick with the wick across the edge of the glass.

4 Add wax to the glass until the cinnamon sticks are covered. Press star anise into the soft wax above the sticks and add more wax.

Candles with Citrus Slices in Water Glasses

1 Cut dried slices of oranges, lemons, grapefruits or cumquats in half with a pair of scissors, and cut the halves into thirds.

2 Pour a thin layer of wax on the sides of a water glass, then press the citrus pieces into the soft wax. Suspend the wick in the glass and fill the glass with melted wax.

Memories: Page for Page Worth Seeing
Pages 12–15

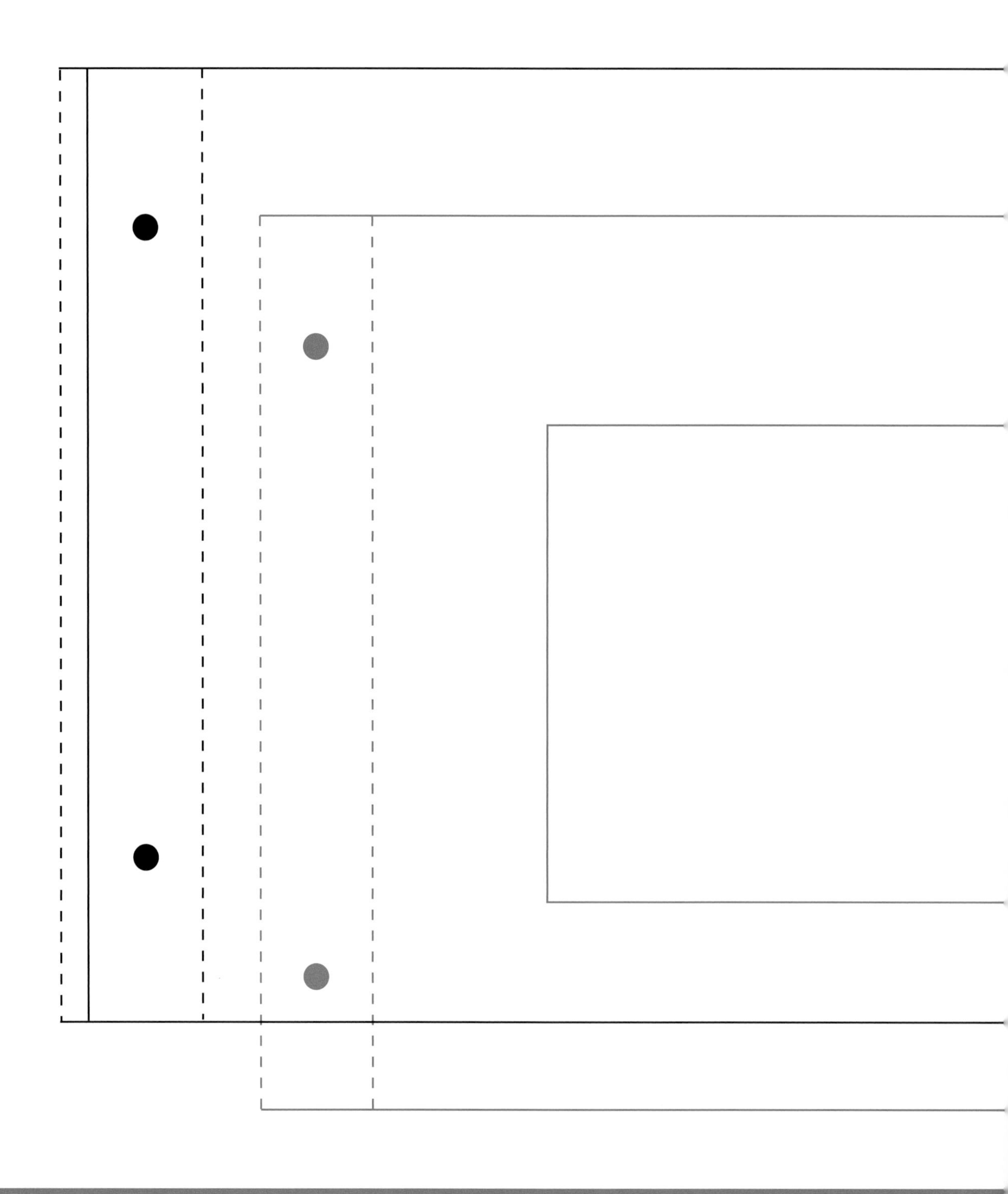

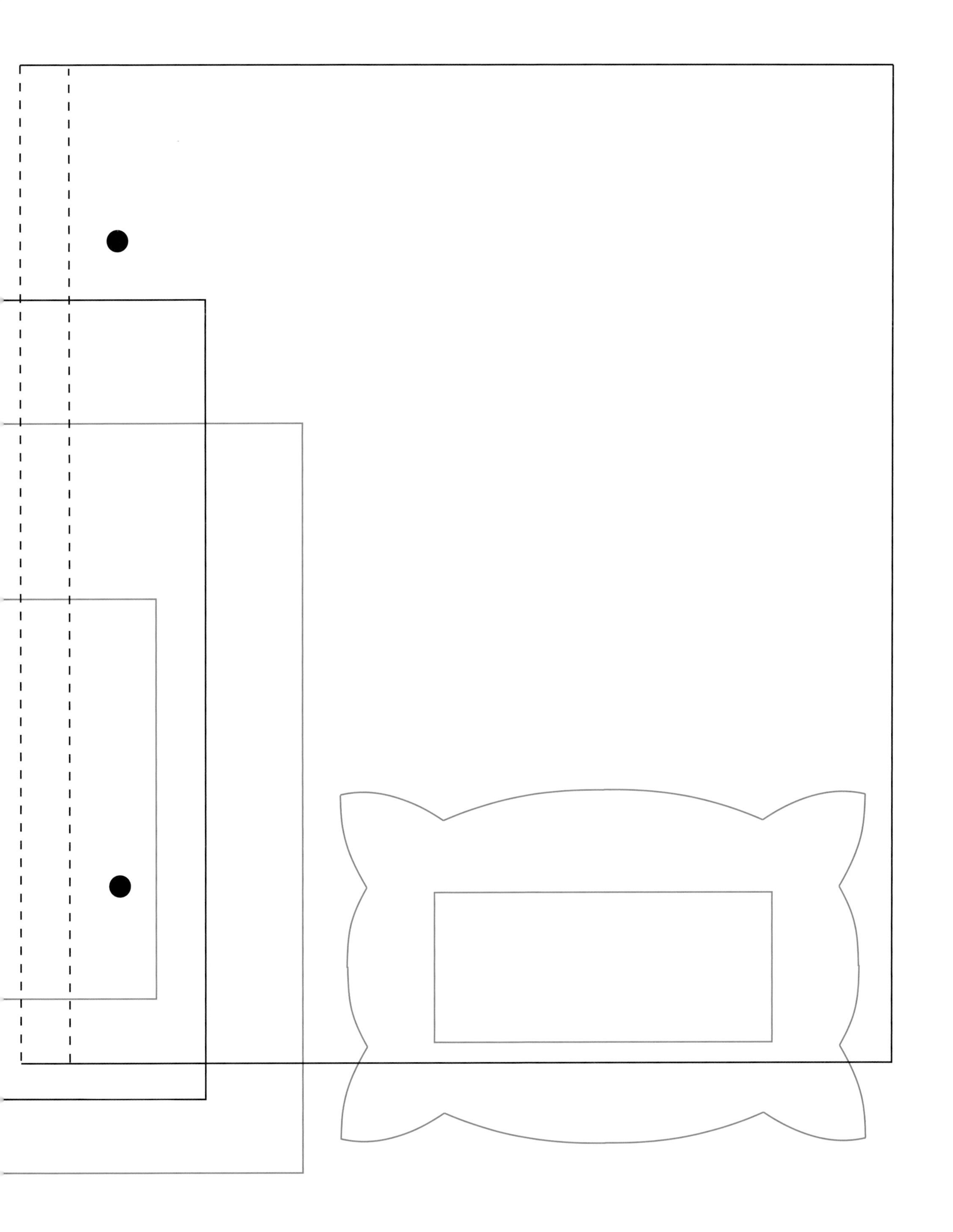

Hand-painted Glasses and Carafes

Pages 32–33

A Personalised Recipe File for Hobby Chefs
Pages 42–43

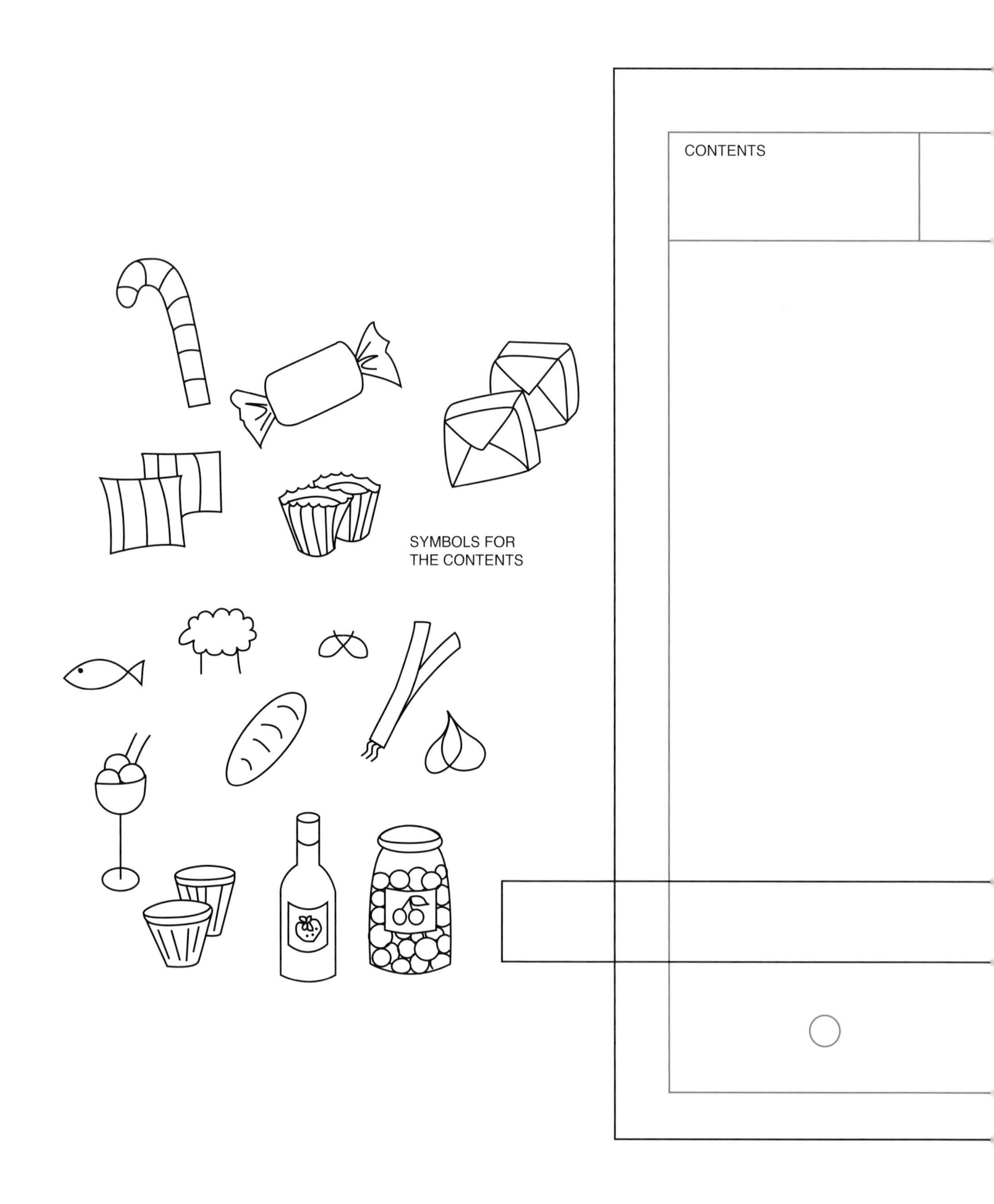

BOOK SPINE

BOOK SPINE

BOOK SPINE

6 8 10

12 16 18

20 22 26

30 32 34

38 40 42

44 48 50